LIFE'S JOURNEY

•

ZUYA

ZUYA

ALBERT WHITE HAT SR.

# LIFE'S JOURNEY

*Oral Teachings from Rosebud*

COMPILED AND EDITED BY *John Cunningham*

THE UNIVERSITY OF UTAH PRESS

*Salt Lake City*

The Defiance House Man colophon is a registered trademark
of the University of Utah Press. It is based upon a four-foot-tall,
Ancient Puebloan pictograph (late PIII) near Glen Canyon, Utah.

LIBRARY OF CONGRESS CATALOGING-IN-PUBLICATION DATA

White Hat, Albert.
Life's journey—Zuya : oral teachings from Rosebud / Albert White Hat Sr. ;
compiled and edited by John Cunningham.
   p. cm.
Includes bibliographical references and index.
   ISBN 978-1-60781-177-0 (cloth : alk. paper)
   ISBN 978-1-60781-184-8 (pbk. : alk. paper)
   ISBN 978-1-60781-216-9 (ebook)
1. Teton Indians—History. 2. Teton Indians—Folklore.
3. Teton Indians—Social life and customs. 4. White Hat, Albert—
Anecdotes. I. Cunningham, John, 1948 Feb. 17- II. Title.
E99.T34W489 2012
978.004'975244—dc23
                                                    2011047654

Index by Andrew L. Christenson.
Drawings by Dave Delgarito.
Frontispiece and color photographs courtesy Jim Cortez.

*I dedicate this book to my relatives and elders
who kept our way of life going when it was against the law to do so.
They did this despite physical and psychological punishment and,
in some cases, institutionalization. Most have passed away, but without their courage,
our way of life would be lost by now. They were the ones I learned from,
who pointed us back to who we are.*

# CONTENTS

*Color plates follow page 170*

$\downarrow$

## EDITOR'S PREFACE

The beginning of this project was deceptively simple. In the spring of 2002, Albert White Hat Sr. and his family were in Colorado at the annual Denver March pow wow. Having known Albert for a number of years, my wife and I went down to the pow wow from our home in Boulder to visit. In the course of our conversation, Albert mentioned that he had a set of videotapes from his class at Siŋ́te Gleśka University. He said that he was looking to hire someone to transcribe the tapes so that he could make a book from his lectures. We'd heard about Albert's course, Lakota Teachings and Health, were interested to see the material, and offered to do the transcribing work for him. It seemed a wonderful learning opportunity and a very fair trade. Over the next few months we transcribed the tapes and that July went up to Rosebud for his sun dance. When I gave the transcriptions to Albert, I mentioned to him that I had some writing and editing experience and would be happy to look over the book when he was done. Albert thought that sounded like a good idea, but offered that it might be better if we worked on it together, and that was that.

At that point it all seemed pretty straightforward, and I assumed three or four trips to his home on Rosebud over six months, maybe a year of work. We'd sit down together and go over each lecture, taking out the *ums* and *ahs*, classroom digressions, and anything else that impeded the flow of his teaching. From transcribing his lectures, I knew there were a few gaps to fill in the existing material, and I also planned to ask Albert to expand these teachings altogether. Simple enough...though nearly nine years ago.

What wasn't straightforward in this work and what I didn't see coming was the impulse to organize and *clarify* this material, a practice Albert describes within as the basic problem with most books about the Lakota edited or written by Westerners. There were the gaps in his lectures to fill in and topics to expand or introduce, and this work took longer than I had foreseen, but the inordinate time it's taken to complete this book is largely on me. Why I ever thought this material needed clarification escapes me today, but I did. Albert and I recorded more than forty hours of Q&A, which I would cut and paste into the existing material, expounding where it seemed necessary, compiling, editing, and discarding at least five drafts.

Eventually, and I hope successfully, it was back to the beginning. There is a saying in the Zen Buddhist tradition, that in the beginning of Zen practice, mountains are mountains and rivers are rivers. After practicing for some time, mountains are not mountains and rivers are not rivers. After that, going further, mountains are again mountains and rivers are again rivers. Following that same arc, this is largely the material we began with—the stories taught by the medicine men on Rosebud, translated by Albert as they taught, and then taught by him at Siŋte Gleśka University after they retired. There are also stories he heard in conversation with elders and others from his own life journey. Essentially, this is the material initially there in his transcribed lectures in the spring of 2002. He's added more stories that came from our taped conversations, from camp gatherings at the sun dance, the Inipi, or around the dinner table. The text is as conversational as we could make it: this is how the stories are and always have been presented. These are Albert's words, in his voice. Any attempt on my part to explain or clarify (in my voice) is long gone. Amazingly, our friendship has endured; throughout our work, Albert accommodated me with uncommon patience, a lot of humor, and an uncompromising vision. Over and over again, he pulled me back from one conceptual dead end or another and pointed me back to the simplicity and wisdom of these stories.

Thinking about this preface, I reread Albert's introduction to his first book, *Reading and Writing the Lakota Language*, and noticed a paragraph, part of which I've included here: "This text is based on personal experience, and [the structure] relies heavily on oral history. Translations I present and stories I tell are controversial. Linguists have reminded me that their research and the records on the language differ from what I present. In the last twenty years I have read the documents and listened to my Elders. I have chosen to teach the oral history along with some selected information from written sources." I've included this passage even though Albert addresses the frequent differences, and resulting controversies, between the written and oral records in his preface. I feel it's important to keep this in mind.

Also, throughout the book, when he says, "They," as in "They say," "They always say," "They said," he is referring to those who told the stories, to oral history. However, other times when he says "They" or "Them," he is referring to spirit relatives. I believe this distinction is clear in context. Often he will refer to "Each creation," or "Every creation," meaning each individual relative of any nation. Again, I believe this is clear in context. There are no, or very few, names mentioned in connection with these stories. This is in keeping with traditional Lakota respect for those individuals and their families.

A few of these stories are repeated in different chapters. When I asked Albert about this, he said that it's important to hear them over and over again. He said that the stories are deep and often make surprising connections not apparent in the first telling. In some instances, Albert makes these connections, while in others he leaves it entirely up to you. In one chapter, for instance, the pipe is for peace, in another it's for health. When I asked him which one it was, he said, "Give it some thought. See what you think."

Last May we were again on Rosebud, and one morning Albert took us to see the land he lived on as a child. Though we've known him for well over a decade, we had never seen this place. We drove southwest from his current home near St. Francis, over paved and then dirt roads, and finally out through a pasture to a bluff overlooking a wide valley. A creek, probably a half mile from the bluff, ran through the middle of the valley, and across the creek was an *L*-shaped stand of tall cottonwoods, which had shaded his childhood home. Inside the *L* was a single smaller tree, maybe an oak, which Albert pointed out and said had been there, the same size, since he was a boy. There's nothing else there now, no sign of past habitation, and from our vantage point, down the valley and across the creek, beyond the old homesite, the Sandhills, green in the spring, rose and flowed over the horizon, behind us the pine-covered hills and oak-forested canyons and creek bottoms of Rosebud. Albert talked about how he used to roam all over that country, in the hills and canyons and out on the plains: how much joy and freedom he had felt. It was where he first heard and lived many of these stories. Standing there with him was a gift.

So these are the stories and the teachings that have come to Albert, from his people, over the course of his life. They are not a definitive portrait of the Lakota—I don't believe there is any such thing—but they are an eloquent and deep body of teachings from the Rosebud

Reservation. I'm happy to have worked on them with Albert. I hope you enjoy them, and I hope you will give them some thought.

*—John Cunningham*

## ACKNOWLEDGMENTS

I want to thank my family for their support and patience in helping me on my journey back to my culture, spirituality, and Lakota way of life. On that journey I want to thank all the relatives who shared stories about our history, way of life, language, tradition, and ceremonies. These relatives were all elderly people, along with others who were medicine men and spiritual leaders. I didn't want to lose this knowledge because of the wonderful benefits and blessings that I have received from it, and I wanted to leave this knowledge not just for my family, but also for relatives who are seeking a way back to their roots and for those who come from other cultures to share our way of life.

With this in mind I sought a way to put this in writing and want to thank my good friend, like a brother to me, John Cunningham, his wife, Cindy, and his daughter, Catherine, who took the time to transcribe my work and to help me to shape this book. My prayer is they will receive the gifts that I have received in the area of good health and good understanding of the phrase *Mitakuye Oyas'in,* "all my relatives." Finally, I want to offer a heartfelt thanks to the University of Utah Press for its interest in my work, for publishing my first book, *Reading and Writing the Lakota Language*, and now this book. Thank you to the University of Utah Press.

—*Albert White Hat Sr.*

I would like to thank Albert White Hat Sr. for giving me the opportunity to work with him on this book. His friendship is my good fortune. Thanks to the University of Utah Press, and in particular to Jeffrey Grathwohl, who offered encouragement early on, and to Reba Rauch, who encouraged and guided us to completion.

Loving thanks to my wife, Cindy, for her patience and support throughout: this book wouldn't have happened without you. Also, to my daughter, Catherine, who read this material and offered clear insight, and to my friend Bill Sheffel, who did the same. I send thanks to my friend Howard Bad Hand, who introduced me to Rosebud and to Albert.

My love and thanks to Gramp and Brien who took me outdoors early on.

Finally, to Chogyam Trungpa Rinpoche.

—*John Cunningham*

## INTRODUCTION

My name is Albert White Hat. I was born and grew up on the Rosebud Sioux Reservation in South Dakota, and except for a brief period
in my early twenties have lived there all my life. In 2009 I retired
after thirty-four years of teaching in the Lakota Studies Department
at Siŋte Gleśka University in Mission, South Dakota.

In the early 1970s, when Siŋte Gleśka was founded, we had a
nurse-training program and saw a need for our nursing students to
know something about traditional Lakota culture in order to connect with and properly treat people who held those beliefs. We asked
our local medicine men if they would come in and teach this material to our students, and, surprisingly, they agreed to do so. They
even formed an organization called the Medicine Men & Associates
to administer this work. In doing this, these men became resources,
not just to students at the college, but also to the public. Along with
their teaching at the college, they also began a dialogue with the
Jesuit community on Rosebud. These discussions took place in a public forum where they shared their visions and how they received

Mapping the roads or path, writing down the roads (to Sičaŋǵu Oyaŋke, the place of the Burnt-Thigh people)

their instructions. They talked about the spirits they worked with and clearly presented how they fixed their altars. They began to help our people understand who they were.

At that time I was teaching school in St. Francis, South Dakota, and was approached by the university to translate for our medicine men. I was fluent in Lakota and spoke pretty good English, and the idea was that they or their helpers (singers and others) would make a presentation to the class in Lakota and I would translate. Some of these men spoke fluent English, others less so, and some spoke only Lakota, but all of them were most comfortable speaking about our culture in our own language. Over the next ten years, many of these men passed away and others moved on to other activities or felt they no longer wanted to teach, and finally, in the early 1980s, the nursing program ended. Our Human Services Department wanted to keep the course that up to then had been taught by the medicine men as a requirement for a degree at Siŋte Gleṡka and hired me to teach the curriculum they had developed.

That course, and the inspiration for this book, was called Lakota Teachings and Health. It was unique in that at least 90 percent of the material was based on oral history. My resources were not books, but what I learned in my time as a translator and from watching video-tapes of our medicine men teaching (most of which are now archived in our library). In general, I don't rely on historical documents unless I can work from the original in Lakota. Also, my entire life I have learned, and continue to do so, from conversations with our elders. While these are my own words unless otherwise noted, what I share with you I learned from these sources.

When our medicine men began to teach this material, probably 90 percent of our people were deathly afraid of it. For nearly one hundred years we had been taught to believe our traditional ways were evil, that we worshiped the devil and were pagans. This was the message we received in our education, and it became the predominant feeling among our people. It was also the reason the medicine men agreed to teach. They were not public people, and most had never spoken openly about themselves or their visions. They held extensive discussions about whether to teach or not, finally deciding to do so. One of them expressed their reasoning when he said, "If we do this, we want our people to understand what Lakota spirituality is and what the ceremonies are about. We want them to understand who our spirits are. If they understand all this, they won't be afraid. There's nothing to be afraid of in Lakota philosophy and rituals."

My goal is that at the end of this book, you'll have a better under-standing of Lakota philosophy and of our rituals and traditions. I hope you will see that ours is a very simple philosophy. It's a very simple story. I am not trying to convince anybody of anything, only to give a better, clearer understanding of our people and the traditional beliefs and systems that are in place in our culture. Hopefully, and importantly, you will see that there is no mystery in our philosophy, that everything we do is reality based. Because of consistent errors in the history written about us over the years and also because of our own cultural sensitivity, I will try to be as careful as possible with the information I have learned from our medicine men and women, from their helpers, and from what I have learned from our elders and experienced myself. There has been so much mistranslation, misinterpretation, mystery, and romance written about us.

I am going to present our rituals to give an understanding of their basic purpose, the essence of which can be expressed most clearly in the phrase *Mitakuye Oyas'iŋ*. This translates as "all my relatives" or "we are all related." It is an often-used phrase in our culture. Our philosophy and way of life are based on it, and I hope you will give it some thought.

Also, consider phrases like *Mitakuye Oyas'iŋ* and the meaning of Lakota terminology in contrast to Western terminology. That is one focus I'd like you to keep in reading this book. Another is the difference between religion and spirituality. Today there is the term *Wakaŋ Taŋka*, which translates as "powerful being." It's widely used, and I think it's a recent term that came out of the church, a description of the Christian God. Our *Mitakuye Oyas'iŋ* phrase means something much different; it describes our relationship with all of creation, that we are all relatives. When the church arrived, we were taught that Mitakuye Oyas'iŋ was evil, a pagan belief, so over the past few hundred years we began to rely on Wakaŋ Taŋka. Some might disagree with me on this, but I hope you'll think about it. So the difference between religion and spirituality is very central to these teachings. We do not have religion, at least as I understand it. We have spirituality. See what you think of this.

This material is mostly the stories of the Sičaŋǧu Oyate, the Burnt-Thigh nation, the people of the Rosebud Reservation. That's who I am. Most of the medicine men that developed this course were

Sičaŋġu as well. I think that if you come to understand us, you'll be able to understand other cultures and philosophies, however different they might be from your own.

Years ago I went to an Indian conference, and one of the presenters, a Hopi, got up to speak. He looked at all of us and said, "There are some Sioux here, Crow, Onondaga, Hopi, Navajo, Ojibwa…and we all know the educational and administrative policies of this country. We've lived under them for years, we've worked under them, and we know that system well. So I'm not going to waste my time talking about any of that; today I'm going to talk Hopi." As he began to explain the childhood development of the Hopi boy into adulthood and the rituals that go along with that, I began to notice that what he was describing was pretty familiar. He was describing rituals that were just like our sweat ceremony, our vision quest, and our sun dance. They were not the same rituals, but they had the same purpose as ours. So I'm hoping that you will experience something similar in reading this book, that in understanding the Lakota people, you will recognize similarities with other nations and come to understand the concept of Mitakuye Oyas'iŋ.

LIFE'S JOURNEY

•

ZUYA

*chapter one*

I GREW UP IN THE '40S

•

1940S HEHAꞤ IMAĊAĠE

I was born in 1938 and grew up in the 1940s in a little community on Rosebud called Spring Creek. It was pretty neat. At that time our transportation was horseback or team and wagon. There weren't many cars on Rosebud back then, and they were all owned by the government and the missionaries. The missionary for our community would come once a month for mass. Our community was very close, and it was a big occasion. We liked any occasion to gather, and even for mass we would all come out. More important, however, we would gather to hear our storytellers.

We had no modern technology in our homes in those days, not even electricity or indoor plumbing, so in the evenings, especially in winter, we'd come back from school and select our storyteller. We had five in our community of around two hundred people. We'd choose which one we wanted to hear that night and go to their home to chop wood, stockpile it, and haul water for the night ahead. Then we'd go to our homes to eat supper and afterward gather at the storyteller's home. By then a space would have been cleared for us, and someone would bring out a sack of Bull Durham tobacco, roll and light a cigarette, and offer it to the storyteller, who would then begin to tell his or her stories. Each storyteller had different stories. My mother was a storyteller, and hers were mostly historical: what happened at Wounded Knee, the Battle of Little Bighorn, and stories of our movement westward over the years.[1] Also, she had stories of our ceremonies and what various medicine men did in them and some others of our Heyokas, or contraries.

Those are wonderful memories for me, lying there with my friends, listening as our storytellers spoke. In those years we grew up speaking our language and hearing our traditional stories. We were not yet fully conditioned to be afraid of our rituals, and we learned about our way of life from those stories. I feel very fortunate that I was able to experience that way of life, even though it turned out to be for a relatively short time.

In those days many of our people were seasonal field workers and in the spring would move from farm to farm, working the crops. We'd do this from spring to fall and then return to Spring Creek after the harvest. The final job of each year, as I remember, was in October, when trucks would come and haul us, maybe twenty-five or thirty families, to Julesburg, Colorado, to pick potatoes. This was an important time for our community, as we were able to prepare for winter with the money made in the potato fields. That was when we bought our winter clothes, and when we returned home we were prepared for winter. We were self-sufficient and took pride in this. We'd hunt through the winter, and we lived well. The farmer we picked for in Julesburg gave us as many potatoes as we could carry away, and I remember one fall my mother brought back thirty-eight one-hundred-pound bags of potatoes. She would trade the potatoes she brought home to our relatives who would come for them and then bring something else to us in return. One year, after all her trading, we ended up with enough potatoes for one meal, but that was fine

1. Wounded Knee Massacre, December 29, 1890.

Power of word and thought

since she regarded it as her contribution to the well-being of the community. My mother didn't set any price for the potatoes; people came and got them and then brought what they had to trade back to us.

We spoke our language nearly all the time. Our community, like many on the reservation, was very isolated. We were barely touched by the outside world. We did have a government day school, but the instruction was poor, and I barely learned anything. We even spoke Lakota to our teacher at school, and this man didn't even speak the language. The school janitor, who was Lakota, would tell us what our teacher was saying and what we were instructed to do. I remember doing a lot of singing; the teacher would play a piano, and we'd sing. Years later when I could read English I had to laugh, because we'd been making up words to the songs, words that sounded like the ones our teacher was singing. Altogether I remember those days as very simple, wonderful, and even exciting times.

This way of life changed in 1953 when we were given the right to buy liquor.[2] It changed for the worse, and it changed fast. That same year, when we went to Julesburg for the potato harvest, there was a lot of drinking and fighting throughout our time there. People spent all their money on liquor; some got stranded and barely made it back home. People came back home with nothing after a month of work. After that fall in 1953, life on the reservation just got worse and worse.

In 1954, when I was sixteen years old, I went into the boarding-school system on the reservation. I stayed five years and graduated high school at twenty, a very angry young man. Everything I was taught about my people in that school was negative. We were savages and worshiped the devil. Everything I was taught about us was bad. I became angry that I'd been born an Indian, which was confusing because I'd had those earlier experiences, and deep down I knew that what I was learning in school was a lie. I had witnessed our sweat lodges as a child and knew they were not evil.[3]

2. The sale of alcohol to Indians had been illegal since the early 1800s, and in 1933 the repeal of Prohibition did not apply to them. In 1953, however, President Eisenhower repealed Indian Prohibition laws in the United States. Indian reservations remained dry unless they opted to permit the possession and sale of alcohol.

3. Our ceremonies were illegal from 1880 to 1978. When I was growing up, our parents kept us from participating in them for our own protection.

By the time I went into high school, our ceremonial practices had gone completely underground. People were punished for practicing them, so after a sweat ceremony the lodge would be taken apart and hidden. As kids we'd ride our horses through the canyons on the reservation, and every now and then we'd come upon a place where a sweat lodge had been held, always in a very isolated area. It wasn't until years later that I understood why these lodges were dismantled and hidden.

Growing up with our language and some of our traditional practices helped me to survive in the years after I graduated high school. It's what I eventually returned to: those things I learned from my mother and my community in Spring Creek.

In those days the entire community took care of the children. If I was playing at a friend's house, and we did something wrong, his parents would discipline us. It was the same at my house: my mother would discipline any kids who were there and misbehaving. News traveled fast, and my mom would usually know that I'd behaved badly before I got home. All of the mothers in our community shared the responsibility for discipline and supported each other in that effort. I remember that clearly; we couldn't get away with anything, and whenever we tried, everyone knew about it. As kids we were welcome anywhere. We could stay at any friend's house, and our parents would never worry about us. In the '40s that way of life still existed on the reservation. That way of life was still very strong, and our language was still strong.

Also, I have danced for as long as I can remember. My mother would make me a dance outfit, and I would dance. There were certain times in the year, during Lent, for instance, that we had to dance secretly. We weren't allowed to dance then, so we'd hold our pow wows in secret. Just like with the ceremonies, however, I didn't know why we had to do this until many years later.

After many years of repression, in the late 1950s I began to hear people speaking of our traditional ways as if they were history. People would talk about how it used to be, and it made me sad and also made me wonder why it couldn't be that way again. Over the next two decades or so, I thought about this more and more and wondered why we couldn't do the same things again. I began to ask around about our ceremonies and learn what I could about them, and finally, around 1980, I built a sweat lodge in my backyard.

The community I lived in thought I was trying to be a medicine man, and my relatives were terrified for me. They thought I was doing something evil. I had no intention or desire to be a medicine man—it doesn't happen that way anyway—but I knew I needed that particular ritual for my well-being. I still have that lodge, and today it's nothing unusual, but at that time it was very controversial. There was no encouragement at all; people said not to do it. By then we were powerfully conditioned to believe what the authorities and the church said. Our people were terrified.

In 1968 I had conducted a survey of our language on the reservation and found that nearly 100 percent of our people denied it. These were fluent speakers, people who had grown up speaking Lakota, and they all said to forget about it, to let it go. They were afraid of anything to do with our traditional culture. That's how bad it had become by the 1950s and '60s. The boarding schools and their curricula and the teachings of the church had terrified us and conditioned us to dependence on outside authority.

*religious freedom issues*

I still see many traces of that today, but it's slowly changing for the better. One hopeful sign is the little ones who are dancing at our pow wows. They dance in a category we call "Tiny Tots." It's great to see these little ones come out and dance, and it ensures these ways will continue. It's a simple process: introduce a small child to the rhythms, and they naturally want to dance. My children started when they were young and then stopped for a while, but they've all come back to it.

Children always need our support. They know how they want to look, how they want to make their outfits, but we have to help them get started. It takes time to make these outfits. I have a dance outfit that I change a little bit every year. I add something or take something away, and I find that if I put my mind to it, then the help I need will be there. They always told me that's how it works. Once I had an old bustle and finally retired it and used those feathers for other things in my outfit. I borrowed a bustle from a nephew and used that but no longer had my own. That year I was dancing at our Rosebud Fair, and a friend came up and invited me to join him at his car. We walked over, and he reached in and handed me a beautiful bustle. He said, "I brought this over for you because that one you're using is kind of small and you need one. Keep it. It's yours."

I believe that if you put yourself into your efforts wholeheartedly, then good things will come your way. An elderly man from Pine Ridge approached me at a pow wow and said how good it was to see me out there dancing. Then he told me he didn't dance anymore and gave me his set of bells, a beautiful set of bells that I still use today. So there is something vital and alive in our culture, in our practices and rituals. It's not history. Today we live in frame houses, we drive cars and cook on gas stoves, but the spirituality, the life, is still there. It's up to each individual, though; it's a choice. If you want to do it, our ways are still there. It might be a struggle to come back to them, but if you keep going, that struggle becomes a worthy challenge. That's my experience anyway.

Once I heard a young boy ask an older friend of his why a certain practice was done a particular way, and the older one said, "Because that's the tradition." That statement really struck me, and I wondered why—why is it tradition? If you don't know the history behind a practice, then the living meaning is lost, and it becomes an empty tradition. There's no feeling or connection except to the form, and it continues only because it's the way it's always been done. It's important to ask why a practice or ritual is done, why it's a tradition, and then to go further and learn how it came to be.

Our people are very lucky to be here. Sometimes I don't know how we survived. After liquor was legalized for us in 1953, within ten years nearly everyone on the reservation was an alcoholic. It happened so quickly that by the late '60s, many people had begun to hemorrhage to death. That illness seemed to come on suddenly, but until some of us went into alcohol treatment programs, we didn't know that it was alcohol that was destroying our health. So much of that addiction and abuse came from a lack of education about alcohol, but all I knew was that it let me be myself. I thought it tasted terrible, but after the third bottle or so, I began to feel really good. Every time I drank, I was able to be myself. I became Lakota and enjoyed speaking my language, singing my songs. Initially, that was the effect alcohol had on me, and on all of us. Very quickly, however, everyone was in terrible shape, and no one knew what to do about it. Alcohol nearly destroyed us all by itself.

My wife is white, and she grew up understanding alcohol. Her father had a small bar cabinet downstairs in his house. My father-in-law would always limit himself, sometimes to two or three beers a year, and that was only on special occasions. He knew about alcohol. He had been educated about alcohol and knew how to work with it, and I admire him for that.

By that time, however, we had so much conflict in our culture, with each other and within each one of us, that we used alcohol as a crutch. We didn't understand what it was doing to us physically. By 1960 we had nearly 100 percent alcoholism among adults on the reservation. Nearly everyone. We're still struggling with alcohol here today, but we have programs now that are available to people if they're willing to use them. I'm just guessing, but I'd say there's maybe 40 percent

4. Alcohol is still a big problem here, even though sobriety has increased somewhat. Without our noticing it, however, drugs came onto our reservation(s), and today they are a bigger problem than alcohol.

sobriety here today.[4] When I think back on that time and then even further back, on events like Wounded Knee, I wonder how we survived. We've come through so much, yet we are still here.

I think it's important to educate our young people about these things. If they know the history, maybe they won't repeat it. This knowledge can make them strong. They will be more cautious than we were, better educated, and much more able to defend our ways. In the past I used that word, *defend*, all the time, and one day a student asked why I didn't say *fortify* rather than *defend*. That right there is the value of an education; if we can become fluent in English and Western thought, it will help us to fortify our own culture and traditions. I believe this more and more as time goes on.

Sometimes when we tell our story, in this case from the Lakota point of view, and look at the origins of our problems, we might point to the church or to the federal government. We might point to the tribal government and the policies that come down from the federal institutions, at the laws that come down from those institutions and how they've affected us. When we do that, if we're not careful, we get accused of bashing Christianity or bashing white people. It's touchy, but it's very hard to explain our current situation unless we explain our history, and as I said, I think it's important to know the history. The first time I told a priest no, said that I didn't agree with him, and began to debate him, one of my sisters thought I was committing a major sin. She was terrified that I would dare to question a priest. Many of my relatives were terrified that I would dare to do that.

Shortly after Vine Deloria Jr.'s book *Custer Died for Your Sins* came out, we had a conference here at Rosebud. One of the presenters at the conference was an Apache from the Southwest, and he made copies of some parts of that book. For many of us, the material in this book, which pointed out where our problems actually originated, was a real eye-opener, and some people said that the author must be an angry man to have brought out so many painful facts that resulted from the government's Indian policies. Many of them took the point of view that Vine was an angry man when all he did was present those policies and their results from an Indian perspective.

*Custer Died for Your Sins* was published in 1969, and at that time we had a new bowling alley in Mission. It had just been built. Most of us on the reservation thought, automatically, it's not for us. We were conditioned to think like that, but then the organizers of our conference scheduled a lunch for us there. I was scared to go there. As an Indian I felt very intimidated walking into such a nice, new place. I felt like it wasn't for me. It wasn't made for me or any other Indians. So we went there for lunch and ate in a hurry and then left.

When we got back to the college, this Apache man was pacing back and forth outside, muttering, mostly to himself. He said, "I don't understand you people," things like that. I didn't know what was bothering him and asked what he was talking about, and he asked me, "What happened today?" I said, "Well, we had the workshop and we ate." He said, "Where?" And I said, "At the bowling alley." So he asked me what happened there. By then there were others standing around, and none of us could figure out what he was talking about. I didn't know how to reply to him, so he finally said, "At your table, what kind of tablecloth did you have?" Someone answered paper. He asked about the plates, and someone else said we were given paper plates and cups. "Were you given silverware?" "No," I replied. "We used plastic." "Did anyone serve you coffee?" Same answer: "No." He asked if there were whites seated near us, and we said there was a table next to us where maybe ten white people sat. "What kind of service did they have?" I told him they had a nice tablecloth. They had chinaware and silver, and a waiter came to their table frequently to refresh their coffee.

He was pretty worked up and asked us what we were going to do, but not one of us had any response to that. Then he said, "You know, I've heard a lot about the Sioux. I've read about you and know your history, and you're telling me you're not going to do anything about treatment like that?"

One man in our group said he might lose his job if we protested, and this Apache guy asked, "Is your job more important than your pride?" And this guy wouldn't give up; he kept coming back at us until we agreed that we weren't going to go back there again. We wouldn't eat there again until they gave us better service. Today that might not sound like much of a response, but back then it was a big step, and we were all worried about what might happen.

The next morning at our workshop one of the directors walked in, and every one of us kind of slid down in our seats, thinking we were all about to be fired. Sure enough, the director began to speak about our protest: "I understand you don't want to eat at the bowling alley anymore. Is that right?" Nobody said anything at first, but after a bit we said that was so. Then the director said, "I heard about this and talked to the manager over there. He wants another chance." We couldn't believe it, and when we went back for lunch later that day, we had a nice tablecloth, chinaware, and silver. Our waiter came to our table often to freshen our coffee. And it's funny now, but I never felt so uncomfortable.

This story really expresses the way things were for us in the '60s. Most of us pretty much accepted the racist attitudes and put up with them, but some others decided to speak out and stand up. Since then things have changed a little bit at a time, but this was one of the first times I remember where we made a point about prejudice and racism in our community. We had never pointed out those attitudes before. After that we began to point out racial incidents more often.

So our recent history is painful, and some of our people ask me why I bring it up. I tell them that, in the first place, it's my life. I grew up in the midst of it and saw many relatives dying of alcoholism. I think it's important to see the whole picture. Our traditions can sustain us, but every now and then it's important to stop and ask why. Why is this tradition done this way, and why is it important? To understand these things is to gain strength. If we understand why we have a naming ceremony, why we have a Huŋka ceremony, an Inipi, an honoring, a memorial, then we will be more sensitive and respectful people. We will better know who we are and why we're here.

# chapter two

# I WANT TO BRING YOU UP TO DATE
•
## HEKTĀKIYE WIĊOUŋ K'Uŋ HETTĀŋ LEHAŋYAŋ UŋHI NAJIŋPI

Now I want to bring you up to date on where we came from and on some specific events that have taken place over time.

According to written records, French trappers entered the Great Lakes area around the early 1600s and began to trap beaver and other fur-bearing animals. Within a few years they had taken most of these animals and tried to move to new territory to the west. On this journey they ran into a group of people they had not previously encountered, and this group stopped them and said they couldn't go any farther. The trappers turned around and went back to the area they'd been in, the territory of the Ojibwa and the Cree, and asked about this new group; who were they? They were told these people were the Nadowessi. As I understand it, in the French language, to make some words plural, *-ux* or *-oux* is added as a suffix. The trappers took this name, Nadowessi, added *-oux,* and called these people the Nadowessioux. Documents from the trappers and the priests that traveled with them indicate that *Nadowessi* means "little snake," or "poisonous snake," and that became the first translated name of this new group to the west, who were the Dakota nation.

A few years ago I heard from an anthropologist in California who is part Ojibwa. She had read my book on Lakota language and became intrigued by this particular account. She did some research and found the word doesn't mean "little snake" or "poisonous snake" but means "people from the snakelike river." There's a river over there that winds around through that country just like a snake, and the Ojibwa called it the Nadowessi River, so the people that lived there, the Dakota, were known as the people from the area of that river. Eventually, the first part of this name, *Nadowes,* was dropped, and we became know as the Sioux. So while the French translation of the Ojibwa name for us was based on a linguistic misunderstanding, the true meaning comes down from Ojibwa oral history. This type of misunderstanding and mistranslation is very common throughout the written records about our people. Most of them were authored by European explorers and priests, and this is one of the main reasons I rely on oral history.

The name Sioux eventually came to describe a group of people living on the plains to the west of the Great Lakes. Under that name are three divisions based on different dialects of the same language, the Dakota, the Nakota, and the Lakota. The only difference among them is in the language spoken by each group: the words used are basically the same, but they are spoken with a *d, n,* or *l* as the first letter, depending on the nation. Otherwise, there are really no differences among these groups.

There are four divisions of Dakota: Mde Wakaŋtuŋ, Waȟpekuṫe, Waȟpetuŋ, and Sisituŋwaŋ. They were the easternmost tribes of our nation living in the area east of the Missouri River in what are now Iowa, Minnesota, Wisconsin, and North Dakota. The name of each division is a description of a geographical location; *Waȟpekuṫe,* for instance, is translated as "shooters of the leaves," as they were a woodland people and hunted in the forests. Today these people retain their original dialect, and their Dakota names are often Anglicized (Sisituŋwaŋ as Sisseton, for example), and their reservations are all east of the Missouri River.

Two divisions of our nation spoke the *N,* or Nakota, dialect, the Ihaŋktuŋwaŋ and Ihaŋktuŋwaŋni. They also lived east of the Missouri River. Today they are called the Yankton Sioux, and their reservations are in South Dakota, Montana, and Canada.

The Tituŋwaŋ (which today has been changed to Teton), now known as the Lakota, had seven divisions called the Oćeti Śakowiŋ, the seven fires or seven council fires. These divisions are the Sićaŋġu, Oglala, Itazipćo, Oohenupa, Hoḣwoju (Mniḳowoju), Sihasapa, and Huŋkpapa. Here the division names describe an incident in a particular group's history: *Sićaŋġu,* for instance, means "burnt thigh" and describes a time when the people had to escape a prairie fire by running through it. *Tituŋwaŋ* means "people of the prairies," and this group lived west of the Missouri, from the river to the Rocky Mountains and from North Dakota and Montana south to Nebraska, northeastern Colorado, and eastern Wyoming. The Black Hills in South Dakota were more or less in the center of Lakota territory. Today all Lakota reservations are west of the Missouri River in South Dakota, though Standing Rock Reservation reaches up into North Dakota.

While that's a very brief summary of the historical makeup and territory of all of our people, and where we live today, my focus in this book is on the oral teachings of the Lakota nation and, even more so, on the teachings of the Sićaŋġu division, the group now living mostly on the Rosebud Reservation.

Oral history translates the name Lakota as "to acknowledge a relative or family member." As I mentioned in my preface, every aspect of our philosophy of life is rooted in the concept of Mitakuye Oyas'iŋ, "we are all related." You can see this expressed in the true meaning of Lakota, and the *D* and *N* dialects hold to this meaning as well. Throughout our culture, on every reservation, in every division or dialect, the focus of our philosophy is always on Mitākuye Oyas'iŋ.

Our language still exists wherever we live. Our language still exists. What has happened, however, is that it has developed what I call subcultures. For example, in the 1950s Rosebud was pretty much equally divided between the Episcopalians and the Catholics. These churches and their missionaries used our language as a method of acculturation and assimilation into the fold.[1] At the time we had fluent Lakota speakers in both churches, but the Catholics taught and spoke Lakota according to Catholic philosophy, and the Episcopalians did the same for theirs. As these two churches had different beliefs, the converts in them didn't get along very well, but before long they had one thing in common: they were both deathly afraid of traditional Lakota philosophy and ritual. Fluent Lakota speakers in both churches spoke the same words, the same vocabulary, and the same sentence structure as always, but the meanings that were put on the words had been redefined according to these two churches and were now different from our traditional meanings.

Our language was one of the main tools used by the government, the schoolteachers, and the church for acculturation and assimilation. This approach was so successful that by the 1950s and early '60s, most of our people had converted to either Catholicism or Episcopalianism. There were very few who were not in one of these two groups, but then a third subculture emerged. This group spoke what I call reservation language; it is based solely on a culture of alcohol, sex, and violence, all of which had become prevalent on the reservation after the legalization of alcohol for Indians in 1953. Again, there was no difference in the sentence structure used by these three subcultures. They all used the exact same vocabulary, but the meanings of the words varied from group to group. One word could easily have three different meanings. This development in our culture created

1. US government policy intended to transform Indian people and culture into Western European–American people and culture.

*religious freedom issues*

confusion that has continued to the present, such that if you don't know our oral history and the way our language has changed, it is very difficult to know the true meaning of our words.

Today we have a reservation slang based on all of these three sub-cultures. In linguistic terminology our language has been bastardized, but many of us are trying to launder it and bring back the true meaning of our words. If you pay attention to some of the terms I use in this book and the meanings I give them, you will see they might differ from what you have heard before. This difference is an important point beyond linguistic concerns, because with different meanings to our words a different picture of Lakota philosophy emerges, and it is the true picture of us.

Reservation slang is very strong today. If I say *makuje,* for example, the traditional meaning is that I'm feeling lazy or listless; I don't know why, but I feel listless. *Makuje* is the word for that feeling. If I'm having a hard time, with my health or in finding a job, I would say *Otehi.* Having a hard time is the traditional meaning of *Otehi.* In 1975 I was teaching our language to seventh and eighth graders in St. Francis.[2] One day I was going over some vocabulary words with them and said *makuje.* One of the kids said that meant a pint. Another said it meant a jug. When I said *Otehi,* another student said it meant that you were in really bad shape. So I asked him what I was saying when I used the word *makuje,* and he said it meant hangover. Now, traditionally *makuje* and *Otehi* used together mean I feel lazy but am not sure why and I'm facing a difficult time, but when I asked my student what the two words meant when used together, he said it meant that you have one hell of a hangover and you've got nothing to sell or hock to get another drink.

That is our reservation slang. Nobody taught those kids those meanings of *makuje* and *Otehi,* but it was what they witnessed, what they saw every day. A parent waking up in the morning with a hangover says, "Boy, *lila* (really, very) *makuje,*" and "hangover" becomes

2. St. Francis, South Dakota, is a small town near where I live on Rosebud. Renamed by the Jesuits, the area was originally called Owl Bonnet. There were always a lot of owls around here, and we have a story of some of our warriors who were coming through this area, pursued by a group from a different tribe. The pursuers were mounted while our warriors were on foot, and it was certain they would be caught. The medicine man traveling with them said to climb to the top of a hill, and he would sing one of his songs and owls would come around. He said that each man should catch an owl and take the *śuŋ apa,* a feather from the head, put it into his hair, and let the owl go. He sang, and the owls came, and each man took the feather. The medicine man said to walk quietly toward the safety of the canyons, and as they did this, the pursuers caught up and rode right past them. They didn't see them. From that event this area was called Hiŋhaŋ śuŋ apa, or Owl Bonnet.

the meaning of that word. When there's nothing left to sell or hock for another bottle, and the child hears *Otehi*, that must be the meaning of *Otehi*. That's how it always happens. Our actions send a strong message. The old saying that actions speak louder than words is true; how we behave and then use language to describe that behavior, that's how our kids come to understand.

So our language went through powerful changes, and this had a correspondingly powerful influence on us. It completely changed our view of ourselves from pre-reservation times. Take a child of four or five out of the home and put him in a boarding school, forbid him to speak his language, and after twelve or fifteen years he will have lost it altogether. He will no longer know who he really is.

Not only did we come close to losing our native language altogether, but our educational system was so inadequate that we were given severely limited educations as well. In fact, the reservation system and the educational system within it were designed to make us totally dependent on authority, secular or religious. A person living in and educated under that system simply couldn't function without outside consent or permission. We were not taught skills to foster independence and self-sufficiency. We were taught to depend on some authorized organization or another.

Our reservation housing program is a good illustration of this dependency.[3] It's riddled with strict rules and policies. The housing authorities might have given you a house, but if the window broke, you weren't allowed to fix it yourself. It had to be done by the housing authority. We were not allowed to do any repairs on our homes. Many times I've seen houses with broken windows or doors off hinges, and I knew there were people in there with the capability to make repairs, but they didn't have permission and wouldn't do so without it. To do any work on your house at all meant filling out forms and estimating costs, and many of us didn't know how to do it, or we just didn't bother. We would simply wait for the housing

3. US Department of Housing and Urban Development.

authorities to get around to making the repairs. Also, the housing system put a limit on who could live in our homes. In our culture it's traditional to have elders living in your home, but under the housing authority it wasn't allowed. Only parents and their children could live under one roof.

That's just one example of how our policies were designed to instill dependence. Study the federal, state, or Bureau of Indian Affairs (BIA) programs, and you'll see they are all designed to foster that dependency. Get a job and no matter how small the salary, you are cut off from any other form of assistance. Often someone on social welfare could be getting three times as much as the salary from an actual job, and as a result many people simply don't even try to work. We weren't prepared for it in any case; we were taught very little in school, and when we graduated our knowledge and our skills were limited.

I graduated from high school in 1959, and my transcript showed me to be an average to above-average student. I had been on the honor roll three times in my last two years in high school, and I thought I was pretty smart. A guidance counselor from the BIA came to our school and asked me what I wanted to do next. I told him I wanted to be an X-ray lab technician. He was really taken aback and suggested I try something like vocational training for car-body repair or house painting. He said, "You people are good with your hands." I held my ground, however, and was given a choice of Los Angeles, Chicago, or Dallas. Now, I had never been off the reservation except a few trips to Valentine, Nebraska, a ranching town about thirty miles away, but I chose Dallas and was sent to Parkland Memorial Hospital, only to find that I could barely speak English, that I knew only the most basic math, and that I had no idea at all of the sciences. I never felt so stupid in my life.

That's how it was for us by the middle of the twentieth century and for any other Indian who went through the boarding-school system in America. We were cut off from our language and culture, given a limited education, and taught to respond only to outside authority. Coming out of high school on the reservation, you didn't know what to do, so you sat there waiting for something to happen. Eventually, our people just lived from day to day, simply reacting to whatever happened.

Only in the past thirty-five years or so have we begun to address the educational system on the reservation. When we began Siŋte Gleŝka University on Rosebud in 1971, probably 80 percent of the high school graduates from the reservation had to attend remedial classes before beginning college. Today our educational system is far from perfect, but we've been making improvements. As I see it, our job as educators and parents is to help our kids appreciate the value of education and encourage them to learn. This isn't easy because many of us never had that experience in the first place, but in the efforts we're making, in going back to the traditional meaning of our language, in recognizing the value of our traditional culture, and in improving the educational system here on the reservation, I believe we have begun to lay the foundation for a better future for our people.

The dependency that characterized our people in the 1950s was really made possible only by removing our children from their homes and placing them in boarding schools, where they were, by design, cut off from any parental influence or any familiarity with our language and traditions. This was a hard time: other than Wounded Knee and similar historical events, I believe the worst time we've faced, as a people, was during the 1950s and '60s. I mentioned that when I was growing up in the 1940s, although we had no real education, we were still somewhat self-sufficient. Most of us were seasonal workers for farmers and ranchers in the region, and we had land. We had a decent life. My parents had 160 acres east of Spring Creek. We had a log house. We owned horses and built corrals for them, and when we weren't away working, we lived simply but well.

Then, during World War II, those of us who were left after the adult men went into the armed services were sent to work in the ammunition depots in Hastings, Nebraska, and Igloo, South Dakota. I was too young at the time, but my older brothers and sisters all worked at the depot in Hastings for three years. When the war ended we returned home and set about repairing our cabin and corrals that had been vacant in our absence. There was open range at the time, but we found our horses and set about rebuilding our homes. About two weeks into this, a man drove up in a pickup and told my brother we were trespassing. He said we had to go five miles to the west, where there was a government school and 40 acres of land for us. We didn't question this—we didn't have the education to even consider the legality of it—and so we packed our wagon and moved out. We moved onto a 40-acre plot and lived in a tent while my brothers built a new log home.

It wasn't until 1978 that I finally understood what had happened to us after the war. I was on the tribal council and in doing some research found that when we were all sent to the ammunition depots, the BIA took over our land under their trust authority.[4] In that authorization there is a provision that if an Indian doesn't utilize his or her land for ninety days, the bureau can decide what to do with it, and during the war, while we were all away, they consolidated our land into range units and leased them to cattle companies with the stipulation that no one live on them. So when we came home from working in the war effort, not only had we lost our homes and our land, but we were forced onto much smaller plots and into much tighter living conditions. This was the beginning of the cluster-housing developments that continue on the reservation to this day.

Cluster areas and cluster housing were not new ideas but simply the last steps in the containment of our people. In 1877, when the boundaries of the Rosebud Reservation were established, it

4. Established March 11, 1824, as the Office of Indian Affairs, this department was renamed the Bureau of Indian Affairs in 1947.

was made up of the entirety of four counties, Todd, Millet, Tripp, and Gregory, and parts of Lyman County, all of which are in South Dakota. Shortly thereafter, this five-county area was divided into three sections (Okaśpe Yamni), as part of the federal government's policy of divide and conquer. First we had been put on reservations, and then the reservations were divided into sections. Evidently, three sections did not provide enough administrative control over Rosebud, because eventually, under the 1887 Dawes General Allotment Act, it was further divided into twenty-one communities. All of this was done for the purpose of increasing control over us.

The process of containment began with the reservation system. At that time the missionaries who were sent to the reservations were given the assignment of converting us to Christianity. They were told to convert us, and when they were initially unsuccessful, they appealed for help to the government agent in charge of the reservation. In response, in 1883, the United States Congress passed a law outlawing all Native religious practices. All of our rituals were made illegal. We couldn't do our pipe ceremony, our healing ceremonies, vision quests, or sun dances. We couldn't do our sweat lodge. All of our rituals were made illegal, and we were punished if caught performing them. In Canton, South Dakota, a small town to the east of Rosebud, there was an insane asylum for Indians, and many of the people sent there were those caught practicing traditional ceremonies. There is one story of a man who was institutionalized for "standing on a hill, half-naked, talking to nobody." The authorities said he was crazy and had him put away when what he had been doing was the *haŋbleċeya* (vision quest). He had been talking to creation. As a result of this law, some of our people took our rituals and ceremonies underground; otherwise, they'd probably be lost to us by now.

In 1968 this law was still on the books, and many of us began a movement to address our educational, political, and spiritual needs.[5] The boarding schools had cut our hair and forbidden us to speak our

5. This happened all across the United States. The Ojibwa in Minneapolis, for instance, organized to get their people who were alcoholics off the streets, partially in response to police brutality against them.

language, and we let our hair grow and started speaking our language in public. We began to do our rituals openly. This behavior terrified most of our people. My own sisters were terrified of these practices and afraid for me. One day my oldest sister invited me for coffee. She sat me down in her kitchen, gave me a cup of coffee, and said, "You've done some things in your life that could possibly send you to hell. Now you're doing something that will send you there for sure." She said this because I was praying with the pipe and going to sweat ceremonies. I understood why she felt that way, and I didn't try to convince her otherwise, but I didn't stop practicing our rituals, either. Ten years later she showed up to support me at a sun dance, though she still kept some distance from the ceremony. Though I had confidence in what I was doing, I still feel bad that I put her in a position of such fear. She was worried about me and afraid that I would suffer in hell after my death.

That fear of burning in hell was held by most of our people at that time, and it was no small thing. If you look at our cemeteries, you'll see there are a lot of graves outside the cemetery boundaries, graves without markings. These are the graves of people caught practicing our rituals, and when they died the church refused to bury them in consecrated ground. They were buried outside as notice that that person was burning in hell, and I can tell you that if you're a young boy or girl and your favorite uncle or aunt is buried outside the cemetery, it will get your attention. It will upset you and make you afraid.

There were many different policies and laws imposed on us to stop our way of life, and they were all in place in the 1960s when we began to challenge the government. In 1973 some of our people took over Wounded Knee, and that drew national attention.[6] Our situation began to get some notice, and finally, in 1978, Congress passed the American Indian Religious Freedom Act. From 1883 to 1978, however, we were not allowed to practice our true beliefs. Sometimes I have to

religious
freedom
issues

6. American Indian Movement occupation of Wounded Knee on Pine Ridge Reservation from February to May 1973.

laugh, even though it's not really funny, but it wasn't until 1924 and the enactment of the Indian Citizenship Act that we were even made citizens of our own homeland. In 1924, after World War I, the government decided we'd sacrificed a great many of our people in the war, so it made us citizens. Again, however, it was the government that told us how much of a citizen we were and what rights we had, and this authority continues today under the BIA.

Throughout all of this history, somehow, we still exist.[7] First it was physical warfare that was used against us, then psychological, but somehow we survived. Obviously, it hasn't been only the Lakota. At one time there were five hundred different languages spoken on this continent and South America. Today there are only thirty that are still strong. Lakota is one of them, but the bastardized language of the three subcultures I described still holds a powerful influence. Today probably 98 percent of our people are influenced by one of these three subcultures. Maybe 2 percent of our people understand the true Lakota language and philosophy. That's why the medicine men, when asked to teach our students, said yes. They said they would "so that our people, whether they accept our ways or not, will begin to understand and will not be afraid."

A few years ago I was invited to a Jewish community in California. It was an anniversary of the Holocaust, and at a ceremony marking the occasion some children got up one by one and spoke about their grandmothers' and grandfathers' experiences. They talked about what their ancestors had gone through, and how they must never forget. I thought about that in relation to our people. It is important and necessary for us to know our history.

As a linguist I do a lot of translating from Lakota into English. A few years ago a group came from Pine Ridge with some documents for me to work on. These documents described a negotiation team from Washington, DC, and from the Red Cloud Agency meeting in the mid-1880s with our people about the Black Hills.[8] They

7. Today it's difficult to understand how close we were to the edge as a culture. Acculturation and assimilation, along with alcohol, had decimated our culture. For instance, one man told me that in 1960, there was only one drum group left on all of Rosebud Reservation. Today, as we are bringing back our traditional ways, that seems hard to believe.

8. The Red Cloud Agency eventually became the Pine Ridge Indian Reservation in 1878.

were trying to convince us to sign over the Black Hills, but Chief Red Cloud said, "The Black Hills [P̄aha Sap̄a] are our *Wizip̄an*." *Wizip̄an* is a Lakota word meaning "a container for your resources." Today we use that word to describe a suitcase because when you travel, it contains all you need.

In these documents Red Cloud told them that if a man or woman was starving and went into the P̄aha Sap̄a, they would come out fully nourished, physically and spiritually. He said, "We can never sell them, but we will lease them to you for seven generations." When asked what he meant by a generation, he said, "If we agree on this, I will be the first generation until the day I die. My son will be the next until the day he dies, then my grandson. It will go like that." By that count we're now in the third generation. By Western measurement, in which a generation is usually twenty or twenty-five years, we're much further along. Red Cloud said, "We will lease it to you for seven generations, and then we want it back," but the government disregarded that agreement and simply took over the Black Hills. That was the stand we took at the time, however.

So we have overcome many obstacles, and we still have many more to go in order to bring back and retain our traditional ways. We have a tribal government today that's very similar to any city or state government, and we have the same breed of politicians as those in Washington. We have our faults like anyone else, but I think it is only fair for people to hear our side of the story, to know what has happened to us over the years. The cumulative impact of these policies on us was so strong that by the 1950s and '60s, many of our people denied their Indian heritage. Families changed their last names so as not to sound Indian. It's not just the Lakota; this happened across the country. I hear the same stories when I visit other reservations.

A few years ago a number of us came together from many tribes across the country, and we shared stories. A Hopi man spoke up and said, "You know, we come from the reservations, and we all face common problems, frustrations, and issues. One of the more recent problems we face is tourists. They will come in, and they love to take pictures and ask questions. If you're an Indian, they think you're an expert." He said, "A woman drove into our village and saw a man sitting on the ground, cross-legged, leaning against a wall with his hat pulled down over his eyes. She stopped her car, got out, and walked up close to take a picture. Finally, she stood in front of him and asked, 'Sir, are you brown from the sun?' The man pushed his hat back, looked up, and said, 'No, ma'am, I'm Jim from earth.'"

That's a humorous story, but it's fairly typical of tourists. When I go into the cities, I get asked whether I still live in a Tipi, whether I still hunt buffalo. When people find I'm from a reservation, they ask questions like that, and I think it's all due to how we're represented in the media. I'm often in Indian conferences or gatherings where we are all fluent speakers of our language(s). We're open with each other and speak with lively humor and expression; if we tell a story, we act it out, but the minute a nonspeaker appears, we quiet down; we lose our enthusiasm and speak in low tones. I saw this happen over and over again, and when I thought about it, I realized I've never seen a picture of a smiling Indian. I think that since that's how we're portrayed, that's how we end up acting. That's the power of the media. That stoic image of us has a lot of power.

If you look at any Indian curriculum being taught today, I don't think you'll get our true story. The situation is not as bad as it once was, but if the sources are books, it will likely be a distorted, if not completely false, story. Our rituals have been dramatized and colored with a mysticism and mystery that are simply false. Our lifestyle has been romanticized, and in many cases we're presented as history. Our cultures are history, and we no longer exist.

Recently, I received a letter from a woman in Denmark asking if she could come and live with us in the Tipi village and ride our horses across the plains. That sounds like fun, so if anyone reading this knows about a Tiƥi village with horses out here on the plains, please let me know and I'll put her in touch with you.

*chapter three*

## OUR ORIGIN STORY

•

## OȚOḰAHE WIĊOOYAḰE

In the beginning was Inyaŋ, and Inyaŋ was in total darkness. Inyaŋ was soft. Inyaŋ was Waḱaŋ. Inyaŋ began creation by draining its[1] blood and from this blood created a huge disk around itself. Inyaŋ called this disk Maḱa, the earth. Half of the disk was land, and half was water. Inyaŋ called the water Mni. The color of Inyaŋ's blood was blue, and Maḱa, Mni, and Inyaŋ got together and separated out this color. They threw it up into the air, and it became Mahṗiya Ṭo, the sky. Then Maḱa said, "It's dark and I'm cold," and Inyaŋ created Aŋṗeṭu Wi, the sun and daytime, to give light and warmth. Then Maḱa said, "It's too bright and too hot," and Inyaŋ created Haŋheṗi Wi, the moon and nighttime, to balance light and darkness.

Then Inyaŋ created Ṭaṭe to give breath to life. Today we call the wind Ṭaṭe. Maḱa said, "I need a covering. I'm naked and I need a covering." So Inyaŋ got together with the others and talked, and then said to Maḱa, "If we give you a covering, you must promise to give it life and nourishment." Maḱa promised to do so, and life began on earth.

1. I use "it" for Inyaŋ because I've never heard anyone address Inyaŋ as male or female.

This life began in the form of grass, plants, flowers, bushes, and trees, and as each new form came in, another need arose. All of creation came together to address each new need and to decide on the next one to come in. As each new being came in, Iŋyaŋ created the other one, just like it, in the universe. For every blade of grass, there is the other in the universe. For every tree, the other one is in the universe. For every being that came in, Iŋyaŋ created the other in the universe.

Draining its blood for each new creation, Iŋyaŋ became weaker and weaker. The last to be created was the Human nation. Iŋyaŋ created Wiŋyaŋ, woman, to be like the earth, to give life and nourishment to all of her children. Iŋyaŋ created Wičaśa, man, to be like the universe, to provide nourishment and protection. The universe and earth create life together; man and woman create life together.

When creation was complete, Iŋyaŋ was dry and brittle and broke apart and scattered all over the world.

Our origin story was recorded for the first time by Dr. James Walker, a physician working on the Pine Ridge Reservation in the 1880s.[2] The medicine men in that area took him under their wings, so to speak, and taught him many of our rituals and healing practices. Eventually, they adopted him as a healer. Throughout this time Dr. Walker kept extensive records of the stories he heard and the rituals he participated in, and then he sent them to the Nebraska Historical Society. The historical society felt that because Walker was not a trained anthropologist, his notes should be edited by someone who was, and that's what happened. Whoever worked on Walker's notes changed much of the content to conform to western European philosophy. This has happened to us repeatedly and is another reason I don't use books for my resources. Lakota philosophy is usually changed in the written record to conform to Western beliefs and understanding.

2. Walker's version of this story can be found in *Lakota Myth*, published by the University of Nebraska Press.

The medicine men told Walker about our relationship with all of creation, and then, in his published work, we have a God, a celestial hierarchy, the basic Christian setup. So if you don't know our oral history, which tells a very different story from Walker's published version, our philosophy is seen as something very similar to Western philosophy. This isn't the case at all. Our traditional philosophy is nothing like western European. As you read these stories, please keep that in mind.

Our origin story begins in darkness. It says, "In the beginning was Inyaŋ. And Inyaŋ was in total darkness. And Inyaŋ was soft. And Inyaŋ was Wakaŋ."[3] Today the word *Wakaŋ* is translated as "sacred" or "holy," sometimes as "great mystery." In Lakota understanding, however, Inyaŋ has the power to give life or to take life. Inyaŋ has the power to build or destroy. Inyaŋ possesses both good and evil; both have power within Inyaŋ. In traditional Lakota understanding, *Wakaŋ* means "power," the power I've just described. Think about this: *Wakaŋ* is a common word today, and the generally accepted contemporary meaning is more in line with Christian thought than Lakota.

Inyaŋ began creation by creating a huge disk around itself and calling it Maka. Half of this disk was land, and half was water. Inyaŋ's first creations were land and water, Maka and Mni. Inyaŋ's blood was blue, and at first all of creation was blue, but then Maka, Mni, and Inyaŋ got together and separated out this color, and it became Mahpiya To, the blue sky. The original term to describe this is *Miye Matokeča*, or "I am different." Today we say *Mahpiya To*, blue sky.

Then Maka said, "It's dark and I'm cold," and in response Inyaŋ created Aŋpe Wi, which is a shortening of *aŋpetu wi*. *Aŋpetu* is daytime and *wi* is the sun, so *aŋpetu wi* is a description of the sun. It's interesting to me that right from the beginning, we, as creation, complain. We're not satisfied. Then Maka said, "It's too bright and too hot," so Inyaŋ created Haŋwe wi (Haŋhepi Wi), the night and the

3. Inyaŋ was Wakaŋ, and Inyaŋ created everything by draining its blood. Every creation comes from the blood of Inyaŋ and so has the qualities of Wakaŋ, the ability to give life or to take life. Every creation is Wakaŋ.

moon, to bring balance. Next Iŋyaŋ created Ťaťe, to give breath to creation. Today we call the wind Ťaťe.

Maka said, "I need a covering. I'm naked and I need a covering." Iŋyaŋ got together with all of creation on that point, and they decided to give her a cover. First, however, Iŋyaŋ told Maka, "If we give you a covering, you must promise to give it life and nourishment." Maka promised to do so, and life began on earth, first in the form of grass and plants and trees. As each creation came into being, another need arose, and with each need, all of creation would get together and decide how to fill that need.

Also, with each creation that came into being, Iŋyaŋ got weaker and weaker. Iŋyaŋ was draining its blood to make each creation and getting weaker as this went on. Throughout this entire process as each new creation came onto earth, Iŋyaŋ created another identical one in the universe. For every blade of grass on earth, there is another in the universe; for every tree, there is another in the universe. The day you were born, the other you was born in the universe. For every being on earth, there is an identical other in the universe.

The last to be created were Winyaŋ, woman, and Wiċaśa, man. Winyaŋ was created first, to be like the earth, to give nourishment to life, and Wiċaśa was created to be like the universe, to carry the power and energy of the universe that, together with the earth, create life. Man and woman work together just like the universe and the earth. After creating man, Iŋyaŋ was dry and brittle and broke apart, scattering all over the world.

Everything on earth became known as Wamakaśkan Oyaťe, the living beings of the earth. Remember, *Maka* means "earth." *Wa* refers to the beings of the earth, and *skan* means "that move," "that have life or spirit." *Oyaťe* simply means "a nation." In the universe there is Wiċaȟpi Oyaťe, and one interpretation of this term that I've heard is *Wiċaśa ċehpi* (man's flesh). So in this particular meaning, *Wiċaȟpi*

*Oyaṫe* addresses the Star nation. We don't have a word for star; we call them Wiċaḣpi Oyaṫe. These two, Wamakaṡkan Oyaṫe and Wiċaḣpi Oyaṫe, represent the beings of the earth and the beings of the universe. On the day you were born, the other you was born in the universe.[4] Whatever you are doing on earth, the other you is doing that in the universe. Occasionally, that other one will send some energy down to you, and whatever you are doing at the time will get a little boost.

When creation was complete, the phrase *Miṫakuye Oyas'in* came into being. *Miṫakuye* means "a relative"; in the first-person usage it means "my relative." *Oyas'in* means "everything." So, *Miṫakuye Oyas'in* means "all my relatives" or "we are all related." This is the most fundamental belief in our Lakota philosophy, that we are related to everything on earth and in the universe. We were all formed from the blood of Inyaŋ: humans, animals, trees, water, air, stones.[5] Everything in the universe, we are all related.

If I have a need or want to give thanks for something good in my life, I will face west and call all the relatives in that direction. I will call them and express my thanks or tell them my need. I'll turn north, east, and south and do the same. Then I will look up and tell the star people and down to tell the earth, our grandmother. If I am asking for help, I will first tell them my problem and then what I am going to do to address it. I will ask them, as relatives, to help me. It's important to tell them what you are going to do to address your need, to take responsibility as you ask for help. I never ask creation to answer my needs or solve my problems; that's for me to do. I simply ask them to help me as I make the effort. If I have a need that can be addressed by another person, that's probably where the help will come from. If it's a medicinal need, help might come from the Plant nation. If I ask a medicine man to help me, a spirit in a ceremony might give it. Help can come from anywhere, but it is important to remember that all beings possess both good and evil, exactly

4. We have an image in our culture, two triangles, one over the other, the top one pointing down, and the two meeting at their apex, like an hourglass. This represents creation into two, one creator into two, male and female. Also, it represents that whatever is on earth, the same thing is in the universe. We use this image all the time in our artwork and our designs. It's a fundamental symbol of our beliefs. The smaller triangles on the top and bottom of the second image are simply an elaboration on the basic hourglass shape. There can be many variations on this, but whatever is on the top will always be on the bottom as well.

5. Our word for stone is *Inyaŋ*. A stone tells me about Inyaŋ, and that spirit of Inyaŋ is in that stone. That spirit or energy in that stone is Inyaŋ. That's my belief. In English when we talk about a rock, pebble, or stone, it describes a lifeless object, so that's what it becomes. It becomes just an object. But to us it's a living relative.

like Inyaŋ, and we must be careful how we ask for help and what we ask for.

• • •

One time in the mid-1970s the medicine men here were talking with members of the Jesuit community. They met twice a month for nearly two years to talk about philosophy and spirituality. Often I would attend these meetings to listen and learn, and in one session a priest who had served on Rosebud and Pine Ridge for more than fifty years stood up and said, "For quite some time you've been telling us you can see and hear spirits. If that's so, tell me then, what does Satan look like?" A medicine man sitting near me nudged his brother-in-law who was sitting next to him and said quietly, in Lakota, "Why don't you tell him? I know he's one of your brothers." Then the medicine men had a discussion among themselves about the priest's question until one of them stood and said, "You really disappoint us with that question. We were hoping you could answer that for us, since you brought him here with you." He continued, "Since I was a child you've taught me about Satan, how evil he is, and you've also taught me about good. Take a look at yourself and at everyone else in this room. In our philosophy everyone has that spirit of good and that spirit of evil in them, and each one of us decides which one we want to develop. It's our decision. It's up to each one of us. There is good and evil in each creation, in the wind, the water, the sky, each one. Look at the water; if we abuse it, it will kill us. Same with the air. Every creation has both good and evil, and if we work with it as a relative, with respect and honor, we get the same back. That's a relative. You know what that's like from working with your friends; you have a wonderful relationship with them. Well, that's what we practice with all creation." That was the explanation our medicine men gave to the Jesuits. Later in that same meeting, one of them said, "We address our needs to our relatives, but we have to keep good and evil in mind all the time. We can ask for an evil thing and receive that too. It's always there. We have to be careful when we make an appeal."

They said that life was wonderful in the beginning. All of the relatives worked together. As time went on, however, they began to abuse each other. They began to kill each other. They began to abuse the earth. The earth sent out warnings that they should stop this behavior, but no one listened. So the earth cleansed herself by shaking violently, and when she was finished, islands had been created. The land of earth had broken up into islands, separating many of the relatives from each other. The children were given another chance, but as time passed the abusive behavior began again. The same things happened. Again the earth sent out warnings to stop this behavior, and again the warnings were ignored. This time the earth called those closest to her inside. She said, "Come inside," and when they did so she said, "This is the last time." She held them safe inside her and began to shake again—the land opened up and swallowed and closed over, opened up and swallowed and closed over. This went on for a time, this cleansing, and when it was over our people, who were inside, were afraid to come out onto the surface.

In our culture we have a trickster figure called Iktomi. After the cleansing Iktomi took the people to the opening that led onto the surface. Three times the people made it to the opening, and each time they were met by a huge buffalo. Three times they got frightened and went back below. Somehow Iktomi got them to go back a fourth time, and this time the buffalo spoke, saying, "Come out. I want to show you something." The people emerged onto the surface, and that buffalo said, "Look to my right. That nation will feed you, give you shelter, and the tools you need." They looked and saw a herd of brown buffalo. Then the buffalo said, "Look to my left. That nation over there will be your spiritual guides." They looked and saw

6. One of my brothers had some in-laws among the Shoshoni people in Wyoming. One summer he went to visit them and said that one evening he went to visit a neighbor. He said it was a nice evening, and he saw some Shoshoni women were sitting in the shade talking. There was a magpie sitting above them making a lot of noise, and finally one of the women got up and chased the magpie away. My brother asked his friend why she did that, and he said, "That magpie was sitting there calling them names." So the magpie must speak Shoshoni. The meadowlark is the one that speaks Lakota. Different birds can speak different languages.

a herd of white buffalo. Today the spot where our people emerged onto the surface after the second cleansing is one of the biggest tourist attractions in the Black Hills. It's called Wind Cave. We call it Wasu niye, "the hole that breathes." It's a national monument.

Other nations had been protected by Maka during the cleansing. When all who were left were back out on the surface, there was a need to set life in motion once again. The relatives decided on a race to determine how this would be done. Essentially, the race was twice around the Black Hills, a total distance of about a thousand miles. When the race began the magpie flew up and landed on the back of the buffalo, which it knew to be a strong runner.[6] Interestingly, even so soon after the cleansing some of the racers cheated, tried to cut across the course, and were disqualified, but the others stayed the course and, with the buffalo in the lead, just before the finish line the magpie flew ahead and crossed first, declaring the race for the *hu nupa*, the two-legged. The two-legged the magpie declared for, though, was not the human but the bear, because the bear has wisdom. To this day we receive instructions and guidance from the bear in our ceremonies.

If you think about our concept of Mitakuye Oyas'in, which means "we are all related," it begins to make sense that an animal or bird or plant, as a relative, could help you. That is what we try to practice in our daily lives and in our rituals. Mitakuye Oyas'in—we are relearning this philosophy today, and an essential part of understanding it is that there is no mystery in our philosophy. There is no mystery, and there are no miracles. Everything we do is reality based. We understand what we are doing, and we understand who we are working with every moment. We are working with our relatives. We all go back to Inyan.

*relatedness*

*chapter four*

## THE *TIOŚPAYE* SYSTEM

•

## TIOŚPAYE ŤA WOOŤE

*T*ioṡpaye is our word for family. It describes our family system. *Ti* means "he or she lives," "he or she lives someplace," and *Oṡpaye* means "a piece out of the whole." So *tioṡpaye* means "a small piece out of the whole" or, in this instance, "a smaller group (out of the whole nation) that lives together." That's our description of a family, though in this case it describes a larger sense of family than the nuclear family of mother, father, and children.

Membership in a *tioṡpaye* is determined by three paths: bloodline, marriage, and adoption. Bloodline is the most important determinant of membership in a *tioṡpaye*. This goes back to our origin story, to Inyan, who began creation by draining its blood. Inyan's blood is in every creation, and this makes us all relatives. Our family system uses this model on a smaller scale. There are no blood-quantum measurements for inclusion in a *tioṡpaye*. The idea of mixed blood came into existence when the reservations were established and was made into law at the time of the Indian Reorganization Act in 1934. Blood quantum or mixed blood was not an issue for us until this time, but when the act was adopted, it held that a person had to be at least one-quarter Lakota blood for inclusion in the Rosebud Sioux tribe, or any other tribe. This measurement did not exist for us before this.

Marriage is the second path to membership in a *tiošpaye*. Every *tiošpaye* is unique and has its own personality and characteristics. People cannot marry within a *tiošpaye*. In some instances, historically, matchmaking was done. We're like anybody else; we want our children to marry good mates, someone who shares similar values, and matches would be made between *tiošpayes*. The couple would be told of the differences in the *tiošpayes*. I would tell my son what he could expect if he went into her *tiošpaye*, and her parents would tell her what she could expect if she came into his. After that they would have to decide if they still wanted to marry, knowing that they would have to choose one *tiošpaye* or the other. If they chose hers, then my son would have to adopt their ways. If they chose his, she would have to adopt ours. Occasionally, a couple wouldn't be able to decide and might start a new *tiošpaye*. In that case they would combine customs from both *tiošpayes* and create new ones, and the new *tiošpaye* would be different from the two they were leaving.

*Huŋka*, adoption, is the third path to membership in a *tiošpaye*. Adoption makes one a full member of that *tiošpaye* and is very important in our culture. We call it *Huŋka* and have a ceremony to make each adoption. If one man adopts another, then the adopted man becomes his K̇ola. Today this is often translated as "friend," but it means much more than that. They say you are lucky if you have one true K̇ola in your lifetime. K̇olas share with and support each other. If a warrior is wounded in battle, the one who will come back to rescue him will be his K̇ola. K̇olas are committed to the point of giving their lives for each other. It goes that deep. A man may have a male or female K̇ola; he may call a woman K̇ola if she is his closest friend. Women have this same type of relationship. When a woman adopts another woman, the adopted one is called *maṡke*. The same ceremony is held for a female adoption. A *maṡke* can be either male or female just like a Ḱola, but the female term for this type of friend is *maṡke*. It's the same level of commitment, and if someone adopts you, you become a full member of his or her *tioṡpaye*.

A friend of mine told me that one time he went to Minnesota with a friend of his to visit his friend's family. When he was introduced to the family, he met four beautiful sisters, and he was immediately attracted to them. The whole family sat down together for coffee, and my friend said he couldn't take his eyes off those girls. His friend's father was very gracious but kept watching him as he kept his eyes on the sisters. After this went on for a while, the father said, "My son is the only boy I have, and I'm glad he has you as a friend. I'm very happy about this, so I'm going to adopt you as a son." My friend said, "I said, 'Thank you,' but deep inside I was thinking, 'Oh, shit.'" His friend's sisters were to become his sisters as soon as he was adopted. This is a humorous story, but it makes a point. I think that man's father was a pretty wise man.

Each *tioṡpaye* had its own system of governance. Customs throughout our *tioṡpayes* were usually fairly similar, though each had its own particular qualities. Within each *tioṡpaye* there would be several leaders fulfilling different functions. There would be a leader for negotiations and to act as a public spokesperson, a leader for warfare, and a leader for hunting. Each *tioṡpaye* had its own medicine men and women, its own midwives. Someone in that *tioṡpaye* would occupy every role necessary for it to function as an independent unit. Each one had traders, herbalists, craftspeople, and toolmakers, and they all worked to help each other. If someone wasn't artistic and wanted a well-made dance outfit, they would go to a relative and tell them what they wanted and have it made, and then they would compensate the one who made it according to their skills and strengths.

Our *tióšpayes* are still here, and they are large, sometimes huge, because of blood relations over the generations. As I have said, each one is set up to provide everything a family member might need, and each one, while slightly different in customs and characteristics, will follow the basic philosophy described in our origin story.

I went to a sweat ceremony in one *tióšpaye*, and the man who led the ceremony, the man who poured the water, said, "Be silent while the first seven rocks come in. Greet each one silently." I went to a sweat in another *tióšpaye*, and the leader said, "It's all right to talk. Go ahead and visit while the stones are brought in." So in each *tióšpaye* things are done a little differently, but the basic customs are the same. In every *tióšpaye*, for instance, we use the pipe. We pray to the four directions. After that there may be slight differences. It's good to know this so that you don't make any assumptions as to how things are done if you go to another *tióšpaye* for a ceremony.

The moment a young boy begins to speak, he's not allowed to converse directly with his sisters or female cousins. A young girl is not allowed to speak to her brothers or male cousins. This avoidance is observed between siblings until they become adults, at which time they may speak directly to each other but always with honor and respect.

A different kind of avoidance is that a girl will never speak her brother's name in public, and a boy will never speak his sister's name in public. You will be teased if you do. In our culture your brothers- and sisters-in-law are allowed to tease and harass you, and they will do so mercilessly if you give them a chance. You are allowed to do the same to them, but everyone is careful about this, as turnabout is fair play. This is the only area where teasing and harassing are allowed in excess, and it has a purpose: it is meant to teach the virtues of fortitude and patience. Later in life you can be sure you will need these virtues in order to survive, and teasing is allowed here to help develop them.

Today there is very little avoidance practiced, though many of us wish we still held to it, particularly among our children. Our kids fight over every little thing that comes up. Brothers and sisters call each other all kinds of names, and our older people wonder what happened to respect between siblings. Traditionally, no one would ever insult a sibling, especially in public.

There is another old story told, and I don't know if it's true or not, about a family that went to a gathering back in the team-and-wagon days. They arrived, set up their camp, and began to settle in when their two children, a boy and a girl, got into a public fight with each other. Without saying a word, the parents broke camp and left the gathering with their children. They felt great shame that their kids behaved in such a way in public. When they got home the boy jumped off the wagon, ran into the house, and came out carrying a rope. He went off down into the canyons while everyone else unpacked. Much later, when he hadn't returned, his parents went looking for him and found he'd hung himself. They say he did that because he brought shame on his parents and sister. I don't know if that actually happened, but the story encourages me to think of respect and to consider just what is respect. Sometimes today you'll hear someone accidentally speak a brother's or sister's name in public, and someone else will say, "Hey, somebody go get a rope," referring to this story and indicating that they broke that rule.

Each *tioŝpaye* is a very powerful unit in itself. Each has a lot of pride. If my daughter was marrying and going into another *tioŝpaye*, the day she was leaving my wife would sit her down and caution her to remember and observe everything she'd been taught. She would be told to act in such a way as to not bring shame on her parents. A man would do the same with his son. He would caution him to live in such a way that would not bring shame on his parents or the *tioŝpaye* he grew up in. Lakota family unity is very strong. There is pride in each family, not so much about being better than others, but in the ability to live well and demonstrate self-sufficiency. We have a saying, "Naƙe Nula Wauŋ," which means "I am always prepared." In our culture it is important to demonstrate the quality of self-sufficiency.

In our family system a Lakota child can have many grandfathers and grandmothers. When I taught in St. Francis, we had a small faculty lounge in our school. I was eating my lunch in there one day, and a teacher, a nun, asked me about a student who kept missing class for his grandmother's funeral. She said he'd been out for three funerals that semester, and it seemed to her that he was lying. She thought a child had only two grandmothers. I asked who it was, and when she told me I said, "Well, knowing him, I'd say he's probably got about three or four more grandmothers. Our system works that way." Children are equally close to all of them, since there's no measurement or distance in these relationships, as there is in Western culture. When a wake takes place for an elder on the reservation, there are a lot of students absent from school. The deceased was likely a close relation to most of them.

Marriage is not permitted within the same bloodline. I think this is common in all cultures. You might become a member of a different *tiošpaye* from your own because a sister has married into it, but you could still marry into hers since there is, as yet, no blood relation there. Since our *tiošpaye* system has been around so long, and they have grown so large, there are problems for our young people. Even in the 1950s when I was growing up, my brothers and I would meet a potential girlfriend and more often than not, our mom would tell us she was a cousin and that we'd have to keep looking. Today it's worse; it's nearly impossible to find somebody on the reservation who's not a blood relation.

A child in our culture has many parent and grandparent figures. Grandmothers taught their granddaughters about what it was to be a woman, and the child's mother would be the role model for those teachings. Whatever the grandmothers were teaching would be modeled by the child's mother. Grandfathers would teach their grandsons the same way, and the child would see his father and uncles living those teachings. Also, we had no word for orphan. A child is never an orphan under this system. There are always other relatives in the *tiošpaye* who will take a child in and give it the same love and care as would have been given by the biological parents. They will teach the same values as the biological parents and will not be regarded by the child or anyone else as any different from the real parents. So a child is never alone under our system. There is no such thing as an only child, either. Any child will have brothers and sisters from other relatives. They are the same as biological brothers and sisters and addressed in exactly the same way. No difference. In the *tiošpaye* system, a child grows up with many brothers and sisters.

Children in a *tiošpaye* are witness to the good and the bad behavior of the members. Children learn about the consequences of mistakes and deliberate acts from this observation. Our children are never punished physically, but adults are, and children learn from witnessing this punishment. Some transgressions carry very severe punishments, and children are told stories of these major crimes as well. Murder is a major crime, as is rape. Lying is also considered a serious offense, usually resulting in the liar being ostracized from the community. We're no different from any other culture in this respect; there are people who commit crimes in every society.

We have many good stories about relationships. Years ago I was thinking hard about the concept of Mitakuye Oyas'iŋ, trying to understand it and what it means to live it. One day we had a gathering and a feast, and I saw a cousin, an elder, sitting by herself. I got some food and went to sit with her, and when I sat down she just started right in with a story. She said that when she and her husband were young they were traveling from Parmalee to St. Francis. In those days it was team-and-wagon travel, and it was a very hot day in July. She said she was so hot and thirsty that sometime in the afternoon she started complaining loudly, "If I had just one relative, just one, I wouldn't suffer like this. I wouldn't be hot, hungry, and thirsty." She said she went on and on like that until they reached St. Francis. That night, when she went to sleep, a man came to her in her dream and said, "We heard you complaining all afternoon, that you have no relatives to help you. The next time you feel that way, remember that your closest relative was there with you the whole time. That's your mother, the earth. Talk to her next time." When my cousin finished relating this story, she told me, "We're never alone. Look around and you see you always have relatives around you."

So the focus in our philosophy is always on relationship. Every member of society is addressed with a relative term such as *uncle*, *aunt*, *sister*, *brother*. We have a term, *Waċekiye*, that means to acknowledge or embrace a relative with honor and respect.[1] When someone addresses another using a relative term, that's *Waċekiye*. A person's name is never used to address them. Every person is given a name at some point in life, and it has a meaning. That name has a vision. It has a goal, a purpose. The only time a person's name is used publicly is to acknowledge an honorable achievement marking progress toward the goal of that name. At a gathering a name will be announced and an honoring song sung to mark that progress toward the goal.

When I was in grade school in Spring Creek, my friends and I started carving our initials on trees everywhere we went. We'd scratch our initials or names everywhere. One evening I went home, and my mom—I don't know how she found out—said, "They always tell us that if you put your name out publicly, it becomes *Ḣuŋwiŋ*." *Ḣuŋwiŋ* is the smell of rotten meat. They say that's what happens to a name that is proclaimed publicly. The next day when I went back to school I told my friends about this, and we went around and scratched our names off every surface we could find. Years later I was thinking about this and wondered why she would tell me that

1. Missionaries translated this word as *prayer*. Under that translation it described bowing and kneeling to a supreme power, which is much different from the original meaning of acknowledging or meeting a relative.

story. I decided it's a way of preventing someone from becoming too egotistical, too self-important.

Sharing is very important in our culture. They always say that if you share freely from your heart, the value of that gift will come back to you four times over. We have no concept of a loan. If someone needs something you have and are not using, it is simply given to them. If you do ask for something, and it is given, then you have to return the value of that gift four times. In our philosophy nothing is free. There is always an exchange.

*circularity*

One time I was asked the meaning of *wealth* in Lakota. In English I believe it means rich, materially rich, to have a lot of material things and money in the bank. One elder told me that the word *Wićozani* means "wealth." Today we translate *Wićozani*, somewhat off-handedly, as *health*, but *Wićozani* means to live a happy, well-balanced life. It means a life of physical and mental health, in balance with creation. That's *wealth* in Lakota philosophy, and every person and every *tiośpaye* tries to reach that level by practicing four main virtues. They are courage, generosity, fortitude, and wisdom.

*Wo'ohiṫika (wo ohiṫika)* is courage or bravery. They say the hardest thing to do is to make a decision and then live it, and this word describes the courage to make decisions about your life. Today we think of courage in a more physical sense, like soldiers going off to war, but it's more than that. It's the courage to make a decision about your life, to make decisions on issues confronting you, and then take responsibility for those decisions. It seems like a simple thing, but think about it. It's very difficult.

*Waćaṅṫognake* is generosity. It means having the ability to put things into your heart because when you do that, you have love and respect for those things. You honor them. Generosity is not just about giving. In Lakota you give to someone because you honor and respect them. Someone is in need, so you help them out of respect. You don't make loans. It's a gift from the heart.

*expanded concept of persons*

They always said that a sincere gift from the heart comes back to you four times. You might have a need, and suddenly something comes along to address that need, maybe a gift from someone you helped previously. However it comes, if you receive a gift from someone, you will give back to them at some point. It might not even be in your lifetime.[2] If someone helps me out when I need it, I might not ever be able to repay them, but my kids will know where that gift came from, and help will be returned. This is how it used to work a long time ago.

They say the worst thing you can do to a person is to pity them. It's a way of putting that person down, putting yourself above them. If you've ever been pitied, you know it feels terrible when someone comes along and says, "Oh, you poor thing." It feels bad, and it makes you feel helpless, like you can't do anything for yourself. So in Lakota philosophy we never pity others.

The greatest gift that you can give is time from your own life. Each of us has our own mission in life, our own goals, yet sometimes we put that aside to help someone else. They say that's the greatest gift because you are taking time from your own life. So generosity is measured in the ways of respect and honor, not pity or looking at somebody as being lower. We care, we respect, we honor. Somebody who needs help is helped out of respect for another human being.

*Wowaćiŋtaŋka* is fortitude, having the strength and endurance to stick to your decisions, to withstand pressure.[3] A student came into my office and told me he was having a lot of problems with peer pressure. He said all his friends wanted to party all the time, and unless he went with them his life was very lonely. He said the only people he hung out with were the elders. He was complaining about this, it was a very real problem for him, and I asked whether he had activities he liked to do—fishing, camping, whatever. I asked him if he thought about going to the mountains and hiking for a few days or learning to ski. He said no, he hadn't thought of that. I told him

2. When we were moved off our land in the 1940s, we were going down the river road in a packed wagon, and we passed by one of my mother's cousins. He asked what we were doing, and when we told him, he offered us a cabin to live in until we could build our own. We lived there for nearly a year. My mother was never able to repay him, but a generation later my brothers and I were able to help his sons when they needed it.

*Concept of Personhood*

3. *Wowaćiŋ* is a noun addressing the mind. *Ṫaŋka* means "big" or "strong." So "big mind, strong mind." Today we define *Wowaćiŋtaŋka* as "fortitude."

that every summer I have a group of young people, college students, come to my place from the East Coast for a week or two of camping and experiencing our life on the reservation. I told him that some of these kids work and save for two or three years to make this trip, but they want to do it, so they take the time and make the effort for it to happen. Talking to him I realized that we, as Lakota people, need to do more of that.

We have a word, *zuya*, which means "life's journey." It's an old word and describes a time when young men would get together and try to set off alone. The first challenge was getting out of camp without being caught, but if that was successful, they were off on their own, usually with just their weapons. They might be gone for days, weeks, months, or in some cases years. They'd pick a direction, east, west, whatever, and head that way to see what they could find. When they returned home, they would come in as fully mature individuals. Sometimes they might bring gifts or things they had learned on their journey. They would have met other people and survived many challenges and on return would be more responsible and wiser.

I told that student in my office that when those young men left on a *zuya*, there wasn't any way to know when, or even if, they would return, that a *zuya* was a form of education, of learning self-sufficiency and responsibility. I also told him that we don't do that sort of thing anymore; we don't venture out like we used to, but it might be a good thing to do, even for a weekend. So fortitude is to make decisions and to be strong with them. Also, *wowaćiṇtaṇka* implies both the physical and the mental: physical conditioning for physical endurance and mental conditioning for psychological endurance. It applies to both aspects of our lives.

We say that if a person practices those three qualities, courage, generosity, and fortitude, they might develop *Woksaṗe*, the fourth major virtue. *Woksaṗe* means "wisdom" and is the result of knowledge and experience combined. They say you can have all the knowledge in the world, but if you have no experience, you really don't know. So experience is a very precious teaching tool for understanding. A person has to experience what is taught and talked about in order to develop wisdom, and there is a lot to learn. Being old doesn't automatically make you a person of wisdom. Someone might be old, but if they haven't lived and experienced a good life, they won't have developed wisdom. Wisdom is in every tradition that we practice. Our people know that and respect a person of wisdom.

Twenty-two *tiošpayes* came onto Rosebud Reservation when it was established. They were all aligned with Spotted Tail.[4] In the research I've done going back to that time, I've found that I'm related to nearly half the people here, and that's just on my mother's side. If I consider my father's side, it's many more than that.

My name is White Hat, but that's not my father's name. My father's father was named Defying Ears, but the government put it on the books as Deaf Ear. He had two brothers, named Flying Hawk and Flying Eagle. When my father was an infant, his father died in an accident. He was digging a cellar when it caved in, and he suffocated. His wife, my grandmother, remarried a man named Tom White Hat, and he raised my father. On my birth certificate I have two names—Deaf Ear and White Hat. When my father was dying, my brother asked him about the name White Hat, and he said, "That man [Tom White Hat] fed me and clothed me and sheltered me, so I'm trying to keep his name in an honorable position." That's when my brothers and I decided to carry that name.

In 1998 I was made a chief.[5] I don't know how to define *chief*. It's not a Lakota term, and it's also a very recent term. Traditionally, a man of that stature was called *nača*, a man of wisdom and achievement. Such a man was said to practice humility to everyone, even to the camp dog, but today *chief* is defined as something like a king or a president. You know, that status is given today because of Western

4. Sįŧe Gleška (Spotted Tail) was a Brule Lakota tribal leader.

5. We had a term, *niǧe taŋka*, which meant "big belly." Such a man would be elderly and would have lived a good life, in service to his people, and would be well respected. He would be well cared for by the people and well fed. These people would not tell people what to do but would live as they always had, and the people could follow if they chose.

influences, and now they've become really important figures—"I'm a chief," you know, that sort of thing.

I was given a war bonnet, but I put it away for a year while I called all my relatives on both sides of the family. I asked them to gather and presented the bonnet, asking if I had their support to wear it. They said yes, so I asked the White Hats if I could use that name as chief. They said I could, so, Chief White Hat. It was necessary for me to get permission from my *tiošpaye* for that to happen. That's how it's done. I believe this is an example of the type of tradition we can still practice. We can still follow most of our traditions. They must have meaning, however; we must put meaning on these traditions in the world we live in today. Also, we can do this in any language, Lakota or English. Actually, much of what we do today is done in English. Most of us speak English better than Lakota.

As many of our traditions are returning, and our rituals coming back, we are fortunate that the *tiošpaye* system is still intact. It's a very effective system, and, as I mentioned, it's based on our creation story when Iŋyaŋ drained its blood to make every creation. All of the love, honor, and respect in a family stems from our creation story. I think that with patience, by my great-grandchildren's time, much of our traditional culture will be back in place. It's a challenge. Many of us alive today are so conditioned by the (recent) past that it's difficult to let it go. Some of us have been able to let go of that, and some haven't. I think that it takes at least two or three generations for a culture to change direction.

*chapter five*

## GENDER ROLES, COURTSHIP, MARRIAGE

•

## WIŊYAŊ NAHAŊ WIĊAŚA ṪA WOOGLAȞE WIOYUSṖAṖI WOȞIĊIYUZE

I want to share a few things that I feel are important in the roles and responsibilities of women and men, particularly women, in our culture. Traditionally, there are specific roles for men and specific roles for women, and these roles address not only sexual differences, but also lifestyle differences and the responsibilities that come with each. There are some things I don't know about women's roles—they keep much of that information to themselves—but I can share the general view.

The Lakota word for woman, *Wiŋyaŋ*, comes from the word *Iŋyaŋ*, which means "in the beginning." In our creation story we saw that Iŋyaŋ began creation by draining its blood (to create), and that the first creation was Maka, the earth. When Maka asked for a covering, Iŋyaŋ made her promise that she would give nourishment to all life. Later on in our creation story, Wiŋyaŋ, woman, was created before Wiċaśa, man, and she was created to be like the earth and to give life and nourishment to life.

In our culture women set their own guidelines, their own rules. They discipline their own members. If a woman breaks their code, the women's society will discipline her. In the same way, if a man breaks the men's code, then the men's society will discipline him. There are certain areas in which women do not allow the men to participate. Women have a lot of medicine specific to them. They have some physical needs that are different from men's and specific medicine to address those needs, and men do not have any participation in this knowledge. Men are never taught about these medicines. The women handle it all themselves. There are medicines for birth control and for abortions, and only the women know about them. There are cultural guidelines around the use of these medicines, and if a woman aborts a child, she is no longer considered a full woman, in the sense that she is no longer allowed to have children after an abortion. Still, some women choose to have abortions and usually will not marry later. They will not have families and support themselves to the best of their ability.

The first time a young girl has her period, her mother, aunts, grandmas, and sisters gather around her and cry with her because that day they have lost a child. After mourning that loss, they shed happy tears because a new member is coming into their society. They welcome her into the women's society.

A woman's education becomes more focused right after her first period, in a practice called *išnati*, or living alone. At the time of a woman's monthly period, she is doing a ceremony within herself, within her body. A ceremony takes place, and the people respect that time. Out of respect for her the spirits will not witness her at that time and will not come to a ceremony if she's there.[1] A special lodge will be put up for this young woman, and the other women in her family cater to her needs. She is not allowed to cook during that time. Also, other women of good virtue will be selected to be

1. Today there is a lot of misunderstanding around this issue.

with her during those days. They will teach her what it means to be a woman, how she must take care of herself. They will teach her the origin story, the philosophy, the traditions and rituals. They will teach her everything about our culture and a woman's role in it.

This educational process takes place over several months. The young woman will continue to practice *isnati* and be taught by her elders. Eventually, these elders will decide that she is ready to enter society as an adult woman, that she understands (her role), and they will end the period of *isnati*. From that time on, that woman is responsible for taking care of herself each month. She will know what to do, and when her time comes will quietly remove herself from any ceremonial activity. Whenever any type of offering is being made or any kind of ceremony is taking place, a woman during her period will remove herself so that the spirits will come. Also, in removing herself like that she will show respect for herself and others, and she would get the same help as those at the ceremony.

A woman has the responsibility to *tiwahe gle*, to establish a home. They said you could tell what a woman was like by how she kept her home, how it looked. I think things have changed a lot today, but in those times one of the strong points in the focus of a woman's role was to bring life into the world and to nourish it in these teachings. Our men would honor that role not only because they honored Maka, but also because this respect had started for each of them in the homes established by their mothers and other women relatives. If a man respected his wife, his mother, his sisters, if he respected and honored them, he would respect and honor Maka, and he would have learned to do that in his home. That's one of the reasons we feel it is so important for a child to be with his or her mother for the first several years of life. They need to have that loving human contact, to acquire that feeling of what it is to be human. A mother passes love to a child and teaches it respect. The child learns that by experiencing it. Though boys were under the care of men after the age of five or so, those first five years with his mother were when he learned to understand feelings, human emotions. If the mother did her job properly, that boy would grow up respecting life and able to handle strong emotions. Every time you hug a child, you pass that nourishing energy on to it, and that child begins to understand love and respect.

If a boy is raised in this way, he will grow up to respect women. If his mother raises him with love and compassion, with understanding, then he will respect women. Men are taught to respect women and to support that concept altogether. Everything a man achieves, every material possession he has, all his wealth goes to his wife. The lodging and any materials he accumulates belong to her. In return she makes a home for him and their children. A man may claim only his weapons and the clothes on his back. If a man doesn't fulfill his duty, a woman has only to put his clothes outside the door of their home. That's the sign the couple is splitting up. If she should be unfaithful or give some other cause for divorce, then in a community gathering he will set up a drum, hit it, and say, "She's free." I don't really know how common divorce was, but in any marriage it would happen only after both sides of the family had worked with the couple to keep the relationship going.

Traditionally, our men took pride in possessing only the clothes on their backs and their weapons. These were the only things a man needed to survive. Recently, I spoke to a class of high school students, and they all said, "No way!" They wanted to know whose name would be on the bank account under that system. Material things play a much stronger role in our lives today, and they've changed the way we live. The concept of equal rights between the sexes comes into play today, whereas it was not an issue in the past. Today some households have two bank accounts, two cars; a man might claim many of the material items in a household. It's really different. Today when you say *tiwahe gle*, the home, the man is usually assumed to be head of it, not the woman. It's very basic in our culture, however, this thing about two people living together to start a home.

Young girls were guarded closely by their families. The older women in the *tioŝpaye* would look after the young girls. They were never allowed to wander around alone. You have to remember that in those days, people were in danger from other tribes who would kidnap a young woman, so they were closely watched and protected.

In courtship a young man would visit a young woman. For privacy he would bring his buffalo robe, and they would cover themselves in that robe and stand under it and talk. I don't know how they could have done that in the summer, but it was a way to get privacy. They would stand under a buffalo robe outside her lodge and talk. You might have heard the term *snagging*, used today to describe getting a girlfriend or boyfriend. Today an idea that refers back to those times is when a man gets a blanket or a quilt in a giveaway, and someone might say, "That's a snagging blanket."

We didn't have an actual marriage ceremony. The closest we came to it was that two people would begin to live together as a sign that they intended to start a family and a life together. When they did that, their parents would hold a feast to celebrate their union and encourage them to be strong together. Also, matchmaking was done by some families. They would get together and encourage a young woman and young man to join together and start a family. I don't know if this was a very common practice, but my mother was matched with my father, and their marriage seemed to work. I know that tradition carried on into the early 1900s. When you consider a practice like matchmaking, it's important to remember that each *tioŝpaye* was different, and parents wanted their children to be in a *tioŝpaye* that had similar practices to their own. One reason for this is that they wanted familiar ground for their children to live in. Another was so their grandchildren wouldn't be confused when they

were in either parent's *tiošpaye*. If the parent's *tiošpayes* had very different personalities, then the grandchildren would have a hard time
adjusting to either.

When a young woman married and came into her new *tiošpaye*,
her sister(s)-in-law would do a ceremony called Šayaᵽi. Today the
word *ša* is used for the color red, but in traditional Lakota it means
"they adorn somebody or dress up somebody."[2] When a young bride
entered her new *tiošpaye*, her sisters-in-law would gather together
with her and hold this ceremony. Today we have bridal showers,
which are held before the wedding, but the Šayaᵽi ceremony is held
afterward. She would be welcomed into the family, into the *tiošpaye*.
There was a similar ceremony for a man if he married and entered a
new *tiošpaye*, though in that case he would be welcomed by his new
brother(s)-in-law.

I've already mentioned the practice of avoidance in our culture.
The avoidance took place between the sexes, between a daughter-
and father-in-law and between a son- and mother-in-law. These two
would never speak to each other directly. In our view this is a practice to show love and respect for each other. It's also a very practical
way to avoid any sort of inappropriate sexual behavior. We lived in
very close quarters, and human nature is human nature; there might
be some attraction, so this code of behavior was created to prevent
it. When you listen to Ikt̄omi stories, you see that he broke every
rule: he fell in love with his mother-in-law, and he fell in love with
one of his daughters. Ikt̄omi did everything he wasn't supposed to
do. We all have Ikt̄omi in us. Ikt̄omi stories teach about that kind of
behavior.

There's a story of a young bride who told her husband to go to her
mother's house and bring back some pots and pans that she needed.
She said her mother would put them out in the kitchen for him. He
went to his mother-in-law's house, and thinking that no one was at
home walked into the kitchen, only to find her there. Stopping short,

2. The color red was most
often used for this adornment, so today *ša* has
come to mean that color.

he looked around to make sure no one else was around, because in our culture you never want to be caught alone with your mother-in-law. At the least it's a cause for merciless teasing from your brothers- and sisters-in-law. He saw no one else around and was about to back out of the kitchen when he noticed a cat lying on the floor. "Cat," he said, "tell my mother-in-law that I came after those pots my wife needs." "Cat," said his mother-in-law, "when my son-in-law comes, tell him the pots are on the kitchen table." This is a funny story, but it illustrates the nature of these relationships. This code of behavior helps to encourage and enforce honor and respect among relations.

I think that today many of our family-system behavioral codes are misunderstood. In the relationship between a man and his mother-in-law, for instance, although they are not to make eye contact or have direct conversation, he will always honor her first with whatever he has. If he is a good hunter, he will offer her the first choice of meat. Today these codes are often misunderstood, often seen as repressive, but I think they work together to create a durable and healthy structure in our family system. They are usually misunderstood because they are considered in isolation and not seen in their place in the overall system. It's all about honor and respect.

• • •

Childbirth is a woman's ceremony. The moment a woman knew she was pregnant, as soon as she knew this, she would select a woman she respected and would ask her to be the one to ioyujuŋ̇ta, "to reach into the mouth of my child." The woman selected would prepare herself over the time of the pregnancy. She would make preparations for the child, maybe a gift, and would pray for it. She would handle herself with care and respect. And then she would be present on the day of the birth.[3] She would be the one to reach into the newborn's mouth to clean it out. She would say a prayer as she did this,

3. They always say, when a woman is pregnant, that a visitor is coming, and if it doesn't like the setting, then it can turn around and go back. Then you have a stillborn child. There is the term *wakaŋyeja*, which today is translated as "a child being sacred," but that's because of the word *Wakaŋ*. It doesn't mean "a child being sacred"; it means that the child comes from the area where a woman releases herself, but the child comes as Wakaŋ̇ (in the true meaning of Wakaŋ that I have already mentioned). That's why the birthplace must be prepared properly. Either that good or evil can be developed, and the first classroom is the home.

and it would be a prayer for that child's development and accom-
plishment in life, so it was important to pick a good woman for this
role. Sometimes I can be very stubborn, and when I was young and
acted that way, my mother would start to criticize her sister-in-law.
This person was an aunt that I really loved, and one day I asked my
mother why she did that. She said, "I should have known better than
to choose her. She's the one who reached into your mouth, and she's
so stubborn I should have known she would intentionally pass that
on to you." It was funny, but my mother was really mad at her. So
Lakota people believe that behavior can be passed on to a child by
this person, and they are very careful about who is selected to reach
into a child's mouth the first time.

The afterbirth, the placenta, is buried. Wherever it is buried is
considered the birthplace of the child. The child will always come
back to that place for replenishment, to be restored. The child will
have a foundation, roots. We call it *otiwoṫa*, our word for "birthplace." Wherever the placenta is buried establishes the foundation
for the child. Some hospitals up here will allow a family to practice
this today. My daughter was allowed to do it, but first the hospital
sent the placenta to the state lab for some tests, and then about a
week later sent it back to her. She buried the placenta and planted a
tree over it. She also arranged for a particular woman to be with her
for the delivery and smudge the room beforehand. So these practices
are still available to us, but we have to take the time to arrange for
them.

Women have a lot of responsibility in our culture. A woman has
a big responsibility. She is the keeper of all of our traditions and is
the foundation of the home. Women learn this at an early age. Years
ago we didn't have all the activities we have today. Today there is so
much to do, a woman is lucky if she can find a few minutes in her
day to do some beadwork or something like that, but this is a modern development. Traditionally, a woman's main task is the home,

making the home nice and livable. She might spend days tanning a buffalo hide for her Tiṗi. She would learn to do that when she was young, and that would enable her to create a home when she was older. I watched my mother tan a buffalo hide once, and it took her several days. She staked it out on the prairie, washed it, scraped it. It was a lot of hard work. Eventually, our women had some modern tools to work with. They used a scythe, a blade, and held it at an angle to scrape and break the grain on the hide to soften it up. The whole process took several days, even with the scythe. Having watched my mother do that, when someone asks me today if I know how to tan a hide, if they're looking for help, I tell them no. It's hard work, and it takes a long time, and tanning was just one part of a woman's work. Keeping the home was her way of life, and the man's job was to make sure she had the materials she needed to do that. His job was to provide anything she needed to have the home she wanted. The home belonged to her.

A woman would never allow a man to bring his weapons into the Tiṗi. The shape and design of the Tiṗi addressed the stars and the constellations. The three main poles address three constellations and make that connection to them. The Tiṗi is also based on the Miṫakuye Oyas'iŋ concept, "all my relations." The point where the poles meet symbolizes that hourglass shape, that whatever is on earth is in heaven, and that point makes that connection. It is based on the concept of Wolakoṫa, or peace, so a woman would never allow a man to bring his weapons inside. They would be left outside the door in a smaller lodge.

So a woman's training started at an early age. Young girls would watch and learn. They would grow into their role by living it. Young men would learn their role in the same way, and they would witness the development of young women and would learn respect for them. They would honor them in their role.

Education through
stories • Wouŋspe

Men and women each had specific roles that complemented each
other. They reinforced each other's strengths. If a woman was getting married and moving into a new *tioṡp̄aye*, her women relatives in
her birth *tioṡp̄aye* would sit down with her and tell her not to forget
what she had been taught. They would tell her to behave in such a
way that she would not bring shame to those who taught her. A man
would be told the same thing if he was moving into a new *tioṡp̄aye*.
"We've taught you," he would be told. "Now show what you've
learned." If the young couple had difficulties between them, then
the father would take his son aside and correct him. He would do
that regardless of who was responsible for the troubles. Her mother
would do the same with her daughter in that situation.

As with our women, our young men would grow up hearing our
stories and learning our philosophy and our origin story. They had
different responsibilities, however, and were taught how to make
and handle weapons and other equipment, how to hunt for food, and
how to butcher. They knew how to make their own clothing. They

would be able to take care of themselves at an early age. As I mentioned in the last chapter, our young men also did what we call *zuya*, a life's journey, when a young man or group of young men go on a journey. These could be long and often dangerous journeys, and when the young man returned, he was held to be fully mature and responsible. The young men who went on *zuya* would often become very strong members of the tribe.

A long time ago, our hunters, when they came back to camp after a hunt, would stop a distance from the camp and howl. People would recognize which hunter it was from the howl, and if it was a good hunter, they might all run to him, knowing he would divide what he had among the people. The first to receive from him would be the needy, those without a man, the elderly, anyone without means to get food. They would be fed first. The hunters would take only what was left after giving to others, but they knew they had the ability to go out again and get what they needed.

When the reservations were established, our young men needed to have something to do. One of those things was to go off to war—World War I, World War II, Vietnam; our young men fought in those wars, and when they went off to fight, our people said, "That's just like the *zuya*." They would go off to another country, they would learn new things, and when they came back, they would have experienced a different life and know more about what is out there. They would bring back that knowledge, just like a *zuya*. So, until recently on our reservations, whenever there was a gathering, the young men would be asked to feed the people. Serving a plate of food was symbolic, but it was a way to carry on that tradition of the young men distributing food to the people. This practice has almost disappeared, and the women are expected to serve. Today you'll see young men sitting at the table eating, while older people are getting their own food and eating in another room. They're not even coming together for a meal. I think we need to start teaching these practices to our young men once again. We need to talk about them and bring them back.

There is a story that I'd like to share that I think is about a *zuya*. I really like it. It's about some men who set off to the south and just kept going and going. I don't know how long they were gone, but it must have been a long time, and when they returned, someone offered them a pipe. They smoked the pipe and described their journey in detail, all the creeks, rivers, deserts, and mountain ranges they had crossed. They described everything in detail and said that eventually they came to a land where it was very hot and humid. They said the trees were tall and the plants were huge with big leaves, and one night they camped under one of these huge trees. They ate a meal and went to sleep, and the next morning they looked up and saw all these little men sitting on the branches watching them. They said it was strange because these little men had tails, and so they figured they'd gone far enough. That's when they turned around and started back home. The name given to these little men was Śuŋka Wićaśa. *Śuŋka* is "dog" and *Wićaśa* is "man," so this name means "manlike dog." Some years later, when the wagon trains were coming through our territory, one of these wagons had a monkey on it. One of the men who had gone to the south saw it and said, "That's what we saw. That's what was looking down on us from the trees." So these guys must have gone all the way down to southern Mexico or Central America.[4] Even today we call the monkey Śuŋka Wićaśa.

So that's an introduction to some of the different roles and training that men and women had in our culture, but when you look at it closely, you see that both men and women were taught many of the same skills. This was so they could survive alone if it was necessary. A woman was taught many of a man's skills, and a man was taught many of a woman's, but still there were women's practices that were only for them and men's that were only for them. Both sexes, however, received very thorough training. They say a woman

4. We traveled great distances from our homeland. Anthropologists often tell us we came from regions where they have found tools similar to ours, but older. I believe those tools were trade items. This is part of a bigger question in anthropology as to why, if we originated where we say we did, we have left no trace of habitation over the millennia. I believe one explanation for this is our burial practice. When our people die, they are put on a scaffold or in a tree. Eventually, the body decomposes and falls to the ground. The badger eats the bones. The family will come back to the area and clean it up, and you will never find any trace that we were there. They say that when a man of wisdom is on the scaffold, his wisdom floats through the air currents, and if you're on the hill fasting, you might catch some of that wisdom. When the missionaries came, they made us bury our dead, and we buried that wisdom as well.

has a natural connection to creation, to the earth. It's always there, and she has only to take the time to make that connection to experience it in her life. Women are born with that ability.

In our culture we say that men's and women's roles complement each other. They support and nurture each other with a lot of respect. I was at a pow wow in the Northeast a few years ago, and one of the announcers asked me to speak with a young man he knew. He said this man was confused, and I introduced myself to him during a break, when the dancers were getting ready for the next round of dancing. This young man pointed to a man, a traditional dancer, who was combing and braiding his wife's hair and said, "If that's a warrior, I don't want to be one." I said, "That's a true warrior. That's what a Lakota man is." The young man said, "I don't think so," so we talked a little, and I told him he needed to look into that, to study it. I hope he did that so he could understand what he had witnessed.

Women are the keepers of our way of life. They are the teachers of our way of life, but in the past hundred years or so, we've lost that understanding. In the boarding schools we were taught that the man was the head of the household, the head of the family, that the man was in control. This isn't the traditional Lakota view, however, and today we've lost our traditional respect for women. I don't think this understanding is gone forever. I think it's like most of our traditional beliefs: they're still here and can still be practiced if we are willing to do so.

*chapter six*

# LAKOTA SONGS AND MUSIC
•
## LAK̇OT̄A OLOWAη

Lakota persons have always tried to look on the positive, on the beauty of their surroundings, and particularly on the positive within. In our way it's important to project that positive view to creation, and a wonderful way to address this is to sing a melody. Sounds come from all of our relatives, from all creation; the wind, the sound of running water, the sound of thunder—they all create music. Anything that has a sound has a rhythm, and Lakota people try to live with that rhythm of life. The earth's heartbeat is the rhythm we try to follow, and our songs are composed with that in mind. We always have a rhythm to match that heartbeat, and our words are carefully chosen to address a positive view. Our traditional songs are mostly concerned with the four virtues. These are the virtues of bravery or courage, fortitude, wisdom, and generosity. The words to our traditional songs come from those four virtues. They express one or more of them.

Our poems, our lyrics, are never just recited. A poem must have melody and rhythm so people can dance to it. Melody and rhythm are beautiful ways of expressing yourself to creation. Singing is a beautiful way of expressing yourself to your relatives and to creation, and as you learn how to do that, sometimes a song will be given to you by one of the relatives. One song (*olowaŋ*) that we have came from the wolf.

There's a story of a small band that was traveling and got caught out in a blizzard and couldn't continue on. Around here blizzards often last many days, and these people were stuck in a little shelter they were able to put together. On the fourth day, in the evening, the weather cleared up. They were finally able to build a fire to warm up, and because the storm was over, and it was still, they noticed that somebody was singing out on the prairie. They decided to go see who it was. They went out and surrounded the singer, and when they came upon him, it was a wolf singing a song. So sometimes a song will be given to us like that. We still sing that song today, and it sounds like the wolf. The melody is almost like a wolf howling; it's the same rhythm, but with words in it as well, and it all came from the wolf.

1. "On the hill" is a term for doing the *haŋbleċeya*, or vision quest.

Sometimes when you're on the hill, a song will come to you.[1] It'll be taught to you, sometimes by the wind, or other relatives around you will give you a song. And then you share it. When someone is selected to be a medicine man, they'll be taught a song, or songs, for their altar. Those songs taught to them will address certain relatives like the eagle, the buffalo, or the coyote, and they will be given by those nations. It depends on what territory you're in. Around here our spirit friends are usually the eagle, the coyote, the spider, and the black-tailed deer. Those are very common spirits around here, and also the thunder spirit. They are all very common spirits that work with the medicine men here. Each medicine man is given a song by the spirits he works with. When I go to a ceremony and look at the altar and the way the Iyeska has fixed it, the items on it will tell me who their spirit friends are. So in that ceremony, you sing songs for those particular spirit friends.

We have other songs that are simply composed. We have professional singers and musicians who compose music. And when they compose a song, they'll bring it to the public, and if it's pleasing, it'll be taken up by the people. Originally, there were seven sun dance songs. Now we have quite a few because the sun dance came back strong in the 1980s, and different singers composed many different sun dance songs. We sing songs from other nations too. There are songs from the Arapaho nation that were brought back here.

So music is a means of expressing ourselves, as it is for everyone. It could be for a good time or a happy time. It could be for addressing a loved one, or it could be a song calling a spirit. We have name-giving songs, naming songs. A song could express your needs or your difficult times to creation. A song can honor a person's achievement. These are called honor songs, and there are several kinds. Honoring songs are usually composed around the four virtues of fortitude, bravery, courage, and wisdom. The wording of these songs will address those virtues to honor a man or woman of achievement. In our culture any achievement you make in life doesn't put you above other people. The more recognition you get, the more humility you practice. If you're among people, you don't put yourself above them. You're one of the people. So achievement doesn't give you authority. It's just that you have some special gift, ability, and you share that with humility, and sometimes songs are made to honor that.

There are pow wow songs, which are social dance songs. We have music and songs composed specifically for pow wows. Today in our pow wows, songs are composed for each different dance category, like the traditional dancing, the grass dance, fancy-feather dancers, for the men. We have women's traditional dancing, women's jingle-dress dancers, women's fancy shawl—they all have their own style of music.

There is a style of singing and dancing that developed recently that is called contemporary. It's a medium-fast song, and these dancers, most of them wear a lot of feathers on their heads. These feathers are called visors. Some wear those, or some have buffalo horns. And their dance style is almost like fancy dancing. It's between traditional and fancy dancing. It's a beautiful dance to watch. They use a lot of paint on their faces. They have their own music too.

And, of course, we have songs for all of our ceremonies: the sweat lodge, vision quest, sun dance, Lowaŋpi—all of them. I'll say more about them later.

We have songs of a woman expressing her love for a man, and they are called *wiośte olowaŋ*, which means "when the women start singing." *Wiośte olowaŋ* . . . these are songs of a woman's love or regard for a man. These are individual songs, while our traditional songs are for social events and for special gatherings.

We have a style of singing called Wiċaglaṫa. It's done by women, and there's a beautiful story of how we got it. They said a man was captured by a group from a different nation but was able to escape. He ran all night, and then at dawn, at daylight, he found a hiding place. He stayed there all day and then at night started running again. On the fourth day of this, he knew he was going to die. He hadn't had anything to eat, and he had no weapons or supplies. He was still being pursued, and he was certain he was going to die, so before he started out on the fifth day he told his spirit, "Before you leave my body, my last request is that you take it to a safe place where the enemy won't mutilate or destroy it. That's my last request." So he started off again, walking and singing his song. They call that *ic'ilowaŋ*. It means "you sing for yourself." He was doing that as he walked, and all of a sudden he heard this woman singing behind him, helping him. He continued walking, and this woman's singing made him stronger and stronger. His energy came back, and when he made it back to his homeland, he turned around to see who was singing, and it was a doe, a female deer. So he went into his camp, and after he had eaten and rested he was given a pipe. After you come back from something like that, the elders will gather to offer you a pipe and have you recount your story. By smoking the pipe, you have to tell the truth in your account. So he told them about this woman singing and that when he turned to see who it was, it was a female deer.

We have a word, *aglaṫa*, which is to praise or to strengthen somebody with your voice, so they called this singer, this female singer who helped this man, Wiċaglaṫa. So woman gives strength and support with her voice, her singing voice. That's when this role of women singing came to us. These singers support the men singers. They give energy and strength to the song. If you've ever heard it, when a drum is singing and all of a sudden the women sing, it really brings a lot of energy to the song. That's Wiċaglaṫa and is the women's role in singing. She's not just standing back there singing; she's sending energy to the song through her voice.

Then there are songs of encouragement, songs of strength, and songs expressing our needs. You will hear the term *hoyewaye* in these songs, and it means "I send my voice." Today we call these songs prayer songs, but I think that's a Christian term. We are not worshiping anything with these songs but are communicating our needs to creation with a melody. Today, because of this misunderstanding, songs are actually composed to sound like a prayer, like a prayer song. Words are translated to sound like Christian prayer, and the people who sing them are thinking of it as prayer when, actually, they are songs of communication, of communicating with a relative. When we're in the sweat lodge, we communicate with our relatives in each direction. We communicate with the Stone people. This communication is expressed with a melody. It's a wonderful way of expressing yourself.

So music plays a role in every part of Lakota life. The type of song I mentioned earlier, *ic'ilowaŋ*, is your personal song. It means "singing your personal song." This is often misunderstood as a death song, but we never sing about death. Life is important to us. It is pre-cious, and we always seek life. If you knew you were going to die, you might sing a song, but it would be a song about going on a journey. You would sing about that journey.

And today we have memorial songs. We never had memorial songs long ago. The songs that were sung for the deceased were used to encourage the spirit to go on a good journey—not to look back, to have a good journey. Today it's different, and our memorial songs kind of remind me of country-and-western songs. They're very sad songs. Your relatives are crying for you; they are looking for you. They convey the idea of mourning and sadness, and if you're not feeling that way already, these songs will really bring it on. Even if you don't speak Lakota, you'd know you were hearing a sad song. And, you know, losing a loved one is sad, and sometimes remem-bering them is sad too; we can't get away from that, but Lakota cul-ture focuses on life. Everything we do is for life. The most important thing a person can do is live fully in a healthy way, and that should be the focus, even in the loss of a loved one. Traditionally, when someone died there was maybe a four- or five-day period of mourn-ing, and then the survivors would be encouraged to move on with life. The songs for the deceased would encourage them to do the same on their spirit journey.

We feel that if you stay in that mood of mourning, it becomes part of your life. And we call that *aya ic'iya*. *Aya ic'iya* is "you pick up a way of life that you can't get rid of," so if you persist in that time of mourning, that becomes your practice, and the spirit will stay around and instill that in you. At that point it's hard to let go, so when somebody dies, they always say, "Be careful of what you say, or do, because you might become that." We encourage going forward.

Of course, there are times you're going to cry. That's a good thing and you should. Release that sadness, but don't do it all the time because it's going to hold you back in your own life. And that's why we have the sweat ceremonies: to cleanse a person of that feeling. They offer you smoke to help you release that heavy sadness, to release that and move on. They give you water as medicine, to give you strength. So those are the common things done around death and the songs that go along with it.

A less common but very old tradition around death that I want to mention is where some families will keep a spirit, Wanaǧi Gluhaṗi, for one year. It's very old. If you do that, you have to have a special place for that spirit. Somebody has to be there with it all the time. That spirit is fed every day, and then at the end of the year you gather the relatives and friends and have one last meal and release the spirit. And then you move on. Traditionally, this is done for only a very few people, for a very special person, a well-loved person who had good influence and good rapport with everybody. Sometimes they want to keep that spirit for at least a year, so people will know the spirit is with them for a while longer. You can talk to the spirit and you feed it, but at the end of a year, you're used to not seeing him or her physically, and then it's time to release it. This is important for the people, and for the spirit, because spirits need to go on with their journey too, and by crying for them we hold them back. They need to go on, and in holding them back, every time we suffer, they suffer too. Every time we have a hard time, they have a hard time too. So you don't want to be too selfish and do that to a loved one. If you love somebody, you want them to be happy, and so you let them go.

If a family does decide to do this, they will tell the spirit their intention, and these days that will usually be at the funeral. You might take a lock of hair and say, "We're going to keep you for a year." Then at the end of the year, you release the spirit. When all of our ceremonies were outlawed, including this one, they created the memorial feast to mark that one-year period. So at the end of the year, a family would hold a memorial feast. The church might do a service in memory of somebody, but the families were actually releasing the spirit in a way that wouldn't get them in trouble. Over time, though, we kind of forgot the spirit keeping, and today it's usually just a memorial feast. Nothing more. We have mostly forgotten that spirit-keeping practice.

· · ·

We have had the drum for a long time. They used regular hides, just a dry piece of hide stretched out on the ground or over a hole. When you lived the lifestyle we had a long time ago, it would have been too hard to cart around a big drum, or any big object. At one time we had to move everything on foot, so they used to raid coyote or wolf dens and raise the puppies. Then they'd become the carriers for our movement. We didn't want to stay in one place too long and destroy the land, so we'd move around a lot. Also, we'd follow the buffalo.

Since people were always on the move, and it was hard to carry anything heavy, we didn't have big drums like today. People might have a hand drum, something small like that, but big drums are recent. The Ojibwa nation said a woman brought the drum to them, and I think we just adopted it. As I said, at one time we just stretched a hide and used a stick to create the rhythm. We've been thinking of bringing that back. A medicine man showed me how to do it. You stretch a dried hide over a hole; it's more resonant that way than just laying on the ground, and then if the hide loosens up, you can put hot rocks in the hole, and the heat will tighten it back up. I don't think there were drumsticks, either, just regular sticks, so this way doesn't give the deep sound of the drums used today. It's a much lighter sound.

We also had the flute, which, as far as I know, has been around a long time as well. One flute player I knew had a wonderful story about a young man who was on a journey and came upon a canyon area where he heard beautiful music. He heard a very beautiful melody. So he followed the sound and came up next to a cedar tree, which was making that music. It was a windy day, and every time the wind came up, it would make music. He looked closely and noticed a woodpecker flying off from the tree. And he saw that the branch where it had been had different holes in it. He sat there watching and every time the wind came, it made that music, so he took that branch, waving it in the wind and blowing on it, but nothing happened. A man came up to him then and said, "If you like that music, we will show you how to make it, but always make sure it has the sound of the goose."[2] And that man blew on the flute he carried, and it sounded like a goose, the northern goose, making that beautiful sound. Then he said, "The next sound, make sure it's the meadowlark." And he played his flute, and it sounded like the meadowlark. He said, "The last one is us…the elk people," and he played the sound of the elk whistling. He made those three sounds and made them into a beautiful song. He did that using only the sounds of the goose, the meadowlark, and the elk.

The flute comes through the elk dreamers; traditionally, they are the ones who can make them. The elk dreamers are also the charmers. They have medicine that will charm the opposite sex, but it's dangerous to give it to somebody. You put that in the food of somebody you love, and that person will never leave you, no matter what. You're stuck with that person for the rest of your life. I don't know what this medicine is; I don't even want to know. These days I don't know if there are many elk dreamers left.

The elk dreamers had their own society, the Heȟaka Okolakičiye. Some flute makers had that skill passed on from their grandfathers. They were elk dreamers who passed the trade on to these younger men. I know people who are third- or fourth-generation flute makers, but they no longer have any connection to ceremonies. It's interesting. They have that gift of elk dreaming, but they don't know

2. Spirits most often approach someone in a human form.

Elk antlers • Hehaká

the philosophy or the spirituality that goes along with it. They just have the gift. They've been gifted by their grandfather or some other relative and had that passed on to them, but because so many of our ways were illegal, many of these men just didn't learn the spirituality or tradition that went along with that gift.

• • •

We have a tradition of public speaking, of skilled orators, though only certain people can pick that up. The rest of us know who they are, so we use them to speak for us. We go to one of them and tell them what we want done, and then they will create a story to fit that need. These people are also our storytellers. Say you want to put on an honoring ceremony, and you have a special gift for the person you are honoring. You tell the speaker what you want to accomplish in the ceremony, and he will create a story along those lines, telling why you want to give this gift to somebody. You might not have said all the things to him that he speaks in his story, but the speaker will have the skills to make it respectful and honoring.

Each of our speakers has certain skills, or a certain style, and people look for the one that fits their needs. Also, some of them might be wonderful speakers but very negative or discouraging people. Others might be angry and create that effect, so people usually look for somebody who's very positive and creates that effect. If you want to get after somebody, though, there are individuals out there who will do that. So you tell them why you want to get after somebody, and they'll add on to that. They'll really embellish. These guys are senators and congressmen today.

• • •

So music and songs are an important part of our way of life. One of our medicine men was a cousin of mine, and he helped me start the sun dance. I knew his dad real well, and he told me that his father always said that each person should have their own song. You can compose your own song or learn one, but you should have a song, and then sing it when you're happy or sad, when you're lonely or angry. Just sing your song, and it will make a difference. So music is always important in that way. Everyone should have their own song. We can all sing.

*chapter seven*

# INTRODUCTION TO OUR CEREMONIES
•
## LAḰOṮA ṮAWIĊOH'Aη YUIYESḰAP̄I

I think our ceremonies have been with us from the beginning of time. They are the same ceremonies, but a few changes have naturally taken place over time. One of them would be in the specific needs we are praying for. Many of those needs might be different from those of two hundred years ago. A change has taken place in the language used—today we speak both Lakota and English. Physical changes have taken place in the clothing we wear to ceremonies, our transportation to and from the ceremony, that sort of thing. The regalia we use has changed in some ways, some of the materials...so physical things, material things, change. The language too...we use both Lakota and English, but those are really the only changes. The basic structure of our ceremonies is still the same as in the beginning.

Our rituals are designed to help us stay focused on Miṯaḵuye Oyas'iη. They also give strength, endurance, courage, or encouragement. Someone might ask for healing or health, for themselves or a loved one. We practice our traditional rites to gain strength and energy for whatever task or goal we have before us. In our way, you make a decision about what you are going to do, and then you ask for help. In the *haŋbleċeya* you go and stand on a hill and tell creation what you are going to do and that you need help. In the sun dance you talk to creation through the tree. You don't pray to that tree alone; you channel your prayers through that tree and tell creation why you are dancing and what help you need.[1]

You might take a loved one to a ceremony and when the spirits come in ask them to heal that person and tell them that in return you will do a vision quest or sun dance. And these rituals, the sun dance or vision quest, they must be done for four years. The first three years are really experiencing the ceremony, and the fourth year is when it is said that you finally understand and pull it all together. Some people dance four years and then say that nothing happened. I've had people say that to me, but when I asked why they were dancing in the first place, they might say, "Oh, yeah, I was praying for my mother, and she got better" or "I was praying for my son, and he's doing much better now." So you don't have to have a big, striking vision or experience in the sun dance or on the hill. Whatever you are praying for is happening all around you. That's where the answer comes from.

Today the word *sacred* is often used in describing our rituals and ceremonies. I have problems with this term. The church tried to compare and relate our rites to their seven sacraments.[2] If you do that and you're not careful, you'll make our spirituality into a religion. Sacred, to me, is perfection. No evil, nothing bad or negative, just perfection. One interpretation I learned in the church is that you have to be in a state of grace to talk to God, to worship God. The idea of worship is really stressed in the church. You bow or kneel to a higher power, and in that way it becomes a mystery. I think this is a way of controlling people.[3] The whole thing has become something mysterious, beyond the reach of ordinary people. Then people have

1. Earlier I mentioned our word *waċekiye* and how today it is translated into English as "prayer." That's what people believe it means, and this takes the relative concept out of focus. Prayer is a way of addressing a higher power that is above you, above all of creation. Traditionally, *waċekiye* means to acknowledge or embrace a relative, to work together with each other with respect, and that's how we work with that tree in the sun dance.

2. Ceremonies that the Catholic Church points to as sacred, significant, and important for Christians.

3. Our word *uŋmaṡike* means "I have a particular need, and I need help with that need." If I come to you and say, "*Uŋṡimalayo,*" all I'm saying is that I need help with a particular need. The church took that word and translated it as "I'm pitiful; have pity on me." Today probably 90 percent of our people think of that as the meaning. Translations like this were very powerful and have contributed greatly to our people being conditioned to dependency on higher, or outside, authority.

to go to those who understand, and those same people give them the answers. It's a controlling mechanism. In our philosophy, however, individuality is very important. Individual dreams and visions are very important, and they have a purpose. They always say that everybody is different. Everyone is unique and has a purpose.

It's interesting today when I talk to the young people who are coming back to our traditions. Sometimes I worry because they are all coming back from a very structured view of religion, the religion of the church, and so they bring that structure and form back to our ways. They take Indian spirituality and make it into Indian religion, with all the usual mysticism and worship and religious laws. They will tell you that if you don't do things a certain way or if you do something wrong, then something bad will happen to you. They don't say what will happen, but they know something will happen and it will be bad. I think this comes from the idea of committing a sin. This is something we learned from the church. It's not part of our traditional philosophy. Sometimes people do intentional harm or commit evil acts intentionally—we know that happens in every society—but a lot of the time what the church calls sin is simply a mistake. It's not evil and wasn't meant to be. To the Lakota a mistake is simply a mistake, and it's one of the ways we learn. We learn from our mistakes and go on.

You may have heard the terms *red road* and *black road*. I saw an article once on some of Black Elk's teachings, and right in the middle of it was a note on the red road to heaven and the black road to hell. That's very common thinking in our culture today, but I'd like to eliminate it. I think the term *red road* comes from the church. I grew up speaking our language in a time when all our ceremonies were illegal. People would go back in the canyons for a sweat ceremony and when it was over would dismantle the lodge and hide it. They knew they would be punished if caught and were trying to protect themselves. After each sweat they'd all get together to eat and share stories. I would be at these meals and never once heard the term *čaŋkuluta* or *čaŋkusapa*, "red road" or "black road."[4]

In our research on these terms we found that Black Elk was a catechist in the Catholic Church. In his time the church had a chart that was very common on the reservation. I knew about it because my father was also a catechist. He died when I was about four years old, but my mother and I used to visit a man called Father Buechel at the mission in St. Francis. I liked to go there because Father Buechel smoked a pipe, and I loved the smell of tobacco. Father Buechel was fluent in Lakota, and while he and my mother would visit, I'd be looking around his office. Hanging on his wall was a chart showing the red road to heaven and the black road to hell. In the late 1800s and early 1900s, this chart was used in the training of Lakota catechists. I've seen a document that said Black Elk used that chart a lot in his teachings, so when Neihardt interviewed him, I think Black Elk might have said, "It's *like* the red road and the black road of the church."[5] Then Neihardt put that statement in *Black Elk Speaks*, as Black Elk saying that if you walk the red road, you believe in one God and go to heaven, and if you walk the black road, you go to hell. *Black Elk Speaks* gives a feeling of heaven and hell in our philosophy, and many other books do as well. Many of these books also portray our rituals as history; the implication is that they no longer exist.

In the Walker papers I mentioned earlier, all of a sudden in the middle of a paragraph, there is a Supreme Being in our philosophy. When I saw that I wondered where it came from. I did some research and saw that he took the word *Sičuŋ* and translated it into "Supreme Being." As I understand it, however, *Sičuŋ* means "leaving your spirit or your influence someplace." If you've ever read a book and got a sense of the author's feelings, then that's something like the meaning. The spirit of the author is in that book. Or it could be that somebody feels your presence when you're not there; that's your *Sičuŋ*. It's not a Supreme Being. Another section in his book talked about

4. There was a time when we had songs called Čaŋkusapa olowaŋ, "black-top songs" or "black-road songs." We'd be driving down the road, singing in Lakota, beating on the seats and dashboard for drumming, and really getting into it. We called these songs Čaŋkusapa olowaŋ. That's the first time I ever heard that term, sometime around the 1950s and '60s. I never heard it before then.

5. John G. Neihardt, author, along with Black Elk, of *Black Elk Speaks*.

how the directions got their colors. It said that Iŋyaŋ was the color yellow, and I wondered where that came from. I still don't know.

I want to clarify some of these terms and concepts, particularly around our ceremonies, to give you a Lakota perspective on them. You can decide for yourself, but I'd like you to see both sides of the picture. I'd like you to consider all of the information in this book that way. Consider the source of the information, how it has come down to us today, and then make your own decisions about it.

If you study our rituals, you find they are very human rituals. There is no mystery in them. If you understand the stories and the philosophy and participate in the rituals, you find that they are very human experiences. You might go to a ceremony, and a spirit comes in and touches you, doctors you. A real medicine man will tell you who that spirit is. He will tell you how that spirit doctored you, and what you must do in return. You know exactly who you're working with. It's not a mystery. Sometimes I see mystery used as a quality of the word *sacred*, but in Lakota there is no mystery in our ceremonies.

We have many more rituals than those known as the seven sacred rites. Many of them have come to us from what in English are called animals. One story tells of a man who was watching a buffalo cow caring for her calf. He was watching it and learning from that behavior, and the Buffalo nation gave him a vision of how to do a ceremony for a young girl moving into another stage of her life towards womanhood. That's where one of our ceremonies, the Awiċa Lowaŋpi, came from, the Buffalo people. The Awiċa Lowaŋpi has been with us since the beginning of time. It's a very old ceremony. So, many of our rituals come from what we know in English as animals, but in Lakota are called nations: Oyate. Suŋg Manitu is the Coyote nation. Ṡuŋka Wakaŋ is the Horse nation. We don't have a word that means "animal" in our language. As I understand it, in English an animal is a second-class citizen that doesn't have a discriminaing mind. In our culture all living beings have such a mind, and in our relationship with them we have learned that they are more in tune with creation than we are. They provide us with medicine and advice and help us in our way of life.

The names of some of our ceremonies reflect the time when our ceremonies were outlawed. *Lowaŋpi* simply means "they are singing." It's a ceremony conducted by a medicine man and generally for healing or help. Our ceremony called Yuwipi means "they wrap something up." It is also conducted by a medicine man, usually for similar purposes. We had to be code talkers because all of our ceremonies were outlawed for nearly one hundred years. If I saw you in the post office, and I knew there were a lot of Christian Indians around, I would say, "Hey, this evening we're going to drink water." You'd know what I meant, and then you'd come to a sweat. When a government agent or a missionary came around and a Lowaŋpi was going on in a home, they'd ask what was going on and be told, "Oh, they're singing," but it would really be a ceremony. That's one of the ways we got around that law.

We have a ceremony called Pᴛe Ṗa Yuslohaŋpi, "pulling the buffalo skulls." *Pᴛe* is "buffalo" and *ṗa* means "head," though in this case "skull." *Yuslohaŋpi* means "they are pulling or dragging something on the ground," in this ceremony the buffalo skulls. This is a men's ceremony, and today it's usually done at sun dances, but traditionally it was done privately. It was a ceremony to ask forgiveness, and usually just the family and a few other close relatives would be there for it. When somebody does that, they will pierce him on the back and attach the skulls to him with a rope. At our sun dance we'll put the skulls on him and turn him loose in an area outside of the circle. Then he'll be out there walking around by himself until he breaks away from the skulls. The purpose of that ceremony is to ask for forgiveness. You invite the people that you want to forgive you for something you've done, and then when you break, you come back to where they are waiting. If they're there to greet you, that means they forgive you. If they're not there, that means they don't forgive you.

They said that pulling the skulls was originally done privately as a stand-alone ceremony, to ask for forgiveness, but when we started doing that ceremony at our dances, we did it in the circle. That was how everybody began to do it when it came back. I want to say that this is a difficult and powerful ceremony, and I noticed that a lot of young guys at our dance were doing it. A lot of them were doing it, and I didn't think they had a real reason, but were doing it mostly for show. That's when I put it outside the circle, away from the other dancers and supporters, and now I notice not so many of them are doing it.

There is a ceremony for adoption. I mentioned this in an earlier chapter; it's called a Huŋka ceremony. It's an old ceremony, and the story I've heard is that one of our *tiošpayes* got into a conflict with a group from the Southwest, a different nation from the Southwest. Eventually, this conflict built up to the point of warfare, so to try to avoid this, they decided to meet one more time. Each group was to bring their most powerful object.[6] What that meant was that each group was to bring their most important, most central, relative. So the Lakota brought the pipe, and the group from the Southwest brought corn and corn pollen. They put these two relatives together on a buffalo skull, on a mound altar with a buffalo skull resting on it, and then sat down to meet. They said that after that meeting, these two nations left as renewed relatives. Instead of fighting, they renewed their relationship; they adopted each other as relatives. That's what I was told about the origin of our Huŋka ceremony, how it came into existence, though today it is based not on conflict, just on the wish to make a relationship with someone.

We have ceremonies for the four seasons. Our word for "season" is *Wičoičaǧe*, a place where life begins again, where new life comes in. *Lečala* is "new." So for every season, new life comes in. There are four of these events, four seasons. The spring equinox is for welcoming

6. I don't like using the word *powerful* here because it gives you the idea of higher and lower power and takes you away from the relative concept.

back the thunder. The month following the spring equinox, we do a wiping-of-the-tears ceremony on p̌ešle (the bald spot) in the center of the Black Hills. This ceremony is done for individuals and families who have lost loved ones and then for any creation that might be in a state of mourning or grief. That way, when the new growth comes in the spring, we, and all creation, will be in a positive frame of mind, looking ahead.[7]

Briefly, after this wiping ceremony in the spring, they go to a place called Iŋyaŋkaǧa, "Iŋyaŋ creating" or "Iŋyaŋ making." They do a ceremony there, take some stones from that place to Pte Saŋ He, Devil's Tower, on summer solstice, and do an annual sun dance there. They said every seventh year all the tiošpayes of the nation must be represented, and the ones that are not there will still observe those days wherever they are.

For the fall equinox there is preparation for the winter season. It's the time for fall harvests and major hunts.[8] It's the time for movement to winter quarters. Fall is when the thunder leaves, and a lot of the ceremonial materials that have to do with wood or trees, tobacco mix, for instance, and some medicine is prepared during the time of winter solstice while the thunder is gone. This is particularly true for the tobacco mix, pipe stems, bows and arrows, and any wood product.

By the winter solstice people would be in place. Winter is time for preparation for the coming new year, the new seasons, and for taking stock. It's a time to share knowledge and wisdom, and a lot of teaching takes place. There were a lot of social gatherings within tiošpayes in the winter. So each season had practices and ceremonies to mark them to prepare for the next.

Another ceremony is specifically for young women who are coming of age. It's called Ṫap̌a Waŋka Yeyap̌i, "throwing the ball." I know just a little about this because it's a women's ceremony. What I do know I heard from a woman from Pine Ridge. She did that ceremony

7. Each tiošpaye would do the wiping ceremony throughout the year as well, depending on the situation. Some might wait a year; others might do it four days after losing a loved one. When a highly regarded loved one is lost, then a wiping is done four days after to bring people back to the public and encourage them to look ahead. If a family prefers to mourn for a year, then they are left alone until that wiping ceremony is done for them.

8. My mother spoke a lot about the North Platte River south of here (Rosebud). The winters were not as severe down there, and there was a lot of game. Certain medicines came from down there. It was a very important river to us.

herself, and I've talked to a few others who did it as well. They have a ball made out of buffalo hide, stuffed with buffalo hair, and painted with personal designs and *tiošpaye* symbols. And what I've heard is that a girl who has come of age will hold this ball, and all the people will stand to the west of her. There will be a medicine man standing behind her with a buffalo skull. She'll hold this ball and say a prayer and then throw it into the crowd. Whoever catches the ball will have those blessings she has prayed for. Then she will throw the ball to the other directions, each time to be caught by someone. So the ball carries that gift for those who catch it. This is her gift to the people.

Our rituals are similar to our other traditions in that each family might do them with a slightly different approach. In the 1970s and '80s, as I worked with a lot of our medicine men as a translator, I began to learn their songs, and then I began to sing for them in ceremony. I saw that each one had a different altar. In order to sing for a particular medicine man, you had to look at the altar and read the signs that were there. When that medicine man fixed his altar, you had to be able to read the symbols he put on it and know which spirit or nation each symbol represented. Looking at the flags, the eagle feather, and other items that were on the altar, you would know which sprits were going to come. Then you would mentally prepare for the songs that needed to be sung for that altar. The singer(s) must understand the symbols of each altar. They must know which songs to sing for which spirit. They must be open to each situation, each altar.

Each one of us approaches learning about ceremony in a different manner. One of my nephews asks a lot of questions. I don't do that. I just watch, and sometimes an explanation will come to me when I least expect it, even though it might be something I've been wondering about for quite a while. I have to make the effort to stay open and be ready, but I find that when answers come to me, they make a lot of sense. My nephew, however, asks question after question: one time we were in a ceremony, and he asked a spirit, "This is a Lakota ceremony. How come you doctor white people, blacks, Navajos, Apaches, so many different nations?" The medicine man said, "They (spirits) want me to tell you that when they come in the room, they don't look at the physical individual. They look into the heart and mind of each individual. They respond to what's in there, not to the physical aspects of that person."

People do want to know how these things work, so there are always going to be a lot of questions. Everyone wonders about these things. When the medicine men would come to the college to teach, we'd discuss our ceremonies openly, and at first I felt uneasy about it. I thought there were some things that shouldn't be discussed. Then, after four or five years, I changed my mind because here were all these guys who actually ran the ceremonies and worked with the spirits, and they were sharing it publicly. I asked them about this, and one said, "If we don't explain who we are and where we come from, people will always be afraid of us. They will always come to their own conclusions as to what we do and who we are. They'll speculate, they'll make up their own theories, and a lot of time those theories will lead to fear. It's better for us to tell who we are and who we work with. Then people won't be afraid when they come to us."

Those medicine men shared a lot with us. I always try to correlate what I heard from them with the old stories, our oral history. I continue to do that with everything I learn from our elders to this day. I've found that one of the best classrooms for me is in a sweat ceremony. People really share in a sweat lodge. One medicine man who came to my place for sweats would always share. He'd say, "Today I'm going to share with you what I learned about the water." Or he'd share what he'd learned about the meaning of the buffalo skull on the altar. Each sweat he'd give us a little lesson on all the objects we use: the pipe, the stones, the sage. Every sweat there would be a lesson. He did this for a number of years, and then, when we started our sun dance, he said, "You know what you're doing now. You don't need me out there, but I'll be around." So he passed all that knowledge on to us. Other elders did the same. I heard one man say that we couldn't just keep our ways secret. He said we had to share because otherwise all of our traditions would die with the elders. He said that without the traditions, our people wouldn't know who they were anymore, what makes us who we are.

Every ritual we have is Wokokiṗe. You could translate that into English as "dangerous." It's not only our rituals; every creation, whether a blade of grass, a tree, a rabbit, a horse, or a human, is Wokokiṗe. And that's because every creation is Wakaŋ. Today *Wakaŋ* is often translated as "sacred," and we tend to put anything regarded as sacred above everything else. We put the pipe above most of creation because of that translation, or we put the sun dance above everything else because of that translation. Sacred is a translation that comes from Christian religion and does not reflect the true meaning of *Wakaŋ*. The pipe and the sun dance, however, are like you and me. They're like any other relative. If I come to you and express my needs to you, you might know just what resources I need and help me with them. In the same way, I go to that sun-dance tree and express my needs to that tree, and it helps me find the resources I need. Or I load my pipe and express my needs to all of creation through that pipe, and the pipe helps me find the resources I need.

The reason they say every creation is Wokokiṗe is that everyone has a good side and an evil side. Every creation has good and bad in it, and in working with them, we might use the wrong energy. It's Wokokiṗe because of who we are and our own good and bad sides. I might stand there with a pipe and be thinking negative thoughts. I might be angry with somebody. I might be wishing something bad against somebody. We all do this, but if I do it with the pipe, then the pipe will make it happen. So when we do our rituals, we have to be very careful of what we think and what we say.

In a recent ceremony, a spirit told us not to load the pipe before everyone arrived for our sweats. We were told to wait until everyone was there and then load it. That way everyone can share their prayers while the pipe is being loaded. This way everyone is included in the ceremony, and everyone will naturally be more respectful. That's how it's done at healing ceremonies as well. Everyone is smudged before the pipe is loaded. The smell of sage really clears the mind. It makes you think things over in a positive way. So before we load the pipe, we take precautions. We tell everyone when we are going to load the pipe so everyone can be included. It's important; I've been to sweats where the pipe has been loaded and is in the lodge, and some people don't know it and start joking around or telling stories. When that happens, someone will always point out that the pipe is loaded. It's a reminder to people to be careful in their thought and their speech.

So the danger, Wokokipe, is really us. We are the danger in our prayers, in our rituals. We have to be careful with the energy we bring to our rituals. We are only human, and all of our rituals reflect that. We participate in our rituals as human beings. We participate in them with our relatives. There is no mystery in it at all.

*chapter eight*

# CEREMONY AND CULTURE
•
# LAḰOṮA ṮOUŊ

I believe every culture has a philosophy and a belief system to live by and that different methods or approaches are created to support those beliefs. Whatever the belief system, however, a way to address it through ritual and ceremony will be developed over time. In order to understand our ceremonies, you have to begin with our origin story and the *tioŝpaye* system. You have to begin there. Some of this will have appeared in earlier chapters, but it's important to tie that information in with ceremony here.

The Lakota people have a very simple statement to express our philosophy, which is Miṯaḱuye Oyas'iŋ, "all my relatives." This concept comes directly from our origin story. And the understanding necessary to live that philosophy starts at birth. They always say knowledge is wonderful, but without experience, it has no meaning or feeling to it. So children see our practices from the time they're little. They watch, and often they experience what they see in order to develop understanding. It begins in the *tioŝpaye* system, which they developed and based on the creation story.

*Tiošpaye* simply means "a small group that lives together." This is our family system, and, as I have mentioned, membership is through bloodline, marriage, or adoption. Marriage or adoption will make you a full member, the same as bloodline. *Tiošpayes* are all different from one another. They all have their own characteristics, their own personalities, and their own ways of doing things, even down to their dialogue, their way of speaking. I might be speaking a phrase, and the neighboring *tiošpaye* might use a little different phrasing to say the same thing. But even though the behaviors and customs are a little different, we all understand each other. Each *tiošpaye* is known for something; some are entertainers, some are known for stability, and there are even some that have a negative influence. They are people that you have to be very cautious of because of the way they behave and the way they do things. We even had a *tiošpaye*, and I think traces of it still exist, that was made up of those who carried all their needs on their backs. This *tiošpaye* (in English they might be called homeless) would visit other *tiošpayes* and would be welcomed and fed. They would bring news from other *tiošpayes* they had visited, and they would be welcomed, but they were lazy. They didn't do any work. You would feed them and visit with them, and they would always know when their welcome was up, because you'd wake up in the morning and they'd be gone. They'd move on to the next *tiošpaye*.

So there are all kinds of people in our nation, and sometimes people say we got our bad influences from Europeans, but like everybody else, we've had them from the beginning of time. Things like jealousy, frustration, cheating, and anger—they are always part of every human being. In order to address these negative behaviors in our *tiošpayes*, certain practices were put in place. The first one is always to come back to that creation story and remember that we come from the blood of Iŋyaŋ, that we are all related to all creation. In order to understand that larger view, however, you must first

practice it in your family, or *tiošpaye*. So in a *tiošpaye* system everybody is addressed with a relative term: *older brother, younger brother,
older sister, younger sister*—everyone.

Your father and all of his brothers are the same to you. It's like
having a whole set of fathers. If your father has sisters, then their
husbands are in that role as well and become Lekši. Today *Lekši* is
translated as "uncle" but doesn't mean the same as it does in English. In our culture uncles are also father figures. *Lekši* is just a
different term (than *Aťe*) used to describe a different biological relationship; the emotional and psychological relationship is the same.

On your mother's side, all of your mother's sisters are just like
your birth mother. Their husbands are like Lekši, and her brothers
are Lekši, just like on your father's side. Their spouses are called
Ťuŋwiŋ. *Ťuŋwiŋ* means "birth woman," and you address her as a
woman who has given birth. *Ťuŋwiŋ* implies that she's just like your
mother. So it doesn't mean "auntie." When English language came
along, we began to have uncles and aunts. Europeans said, "Well,
that's just like an uncle and aunt," but the psychological distance
that is implied in uncle and aunt just isn't there in our culture. As
I mentioned earlier, in our family system, if anything happens to
your natural parents, there will be another set of parents to step in.
They will give you the same love and care as their natural children.
We have no concept, or word, for "orphan" in Lakota. Our children
always have several couples as parents, any of whom would take
them in and raise them without question. A child grows up knowing them all and would not feel strange or lonely if raised by someone other than natural parents. A boy has role models in his father,
his father's brothers, his cousins, a girl in her mother, her mother's
sisters, and cousins.

So our *tiošpaye* system was put in place to practice the idea of
relationship. We are all related, and we try to base our behavior on
the four virtues of fortitude, generosity, bravery, and wisdom. They

are the virtues we try to live by the best we can, you know, in the way of honor, respect, and love. So when we use relative terms, when I address a sibling with a relative term, I draw respect. If I call you Misuŋ, as a younger brother you're going to look at me as an older brother, and automatically there will be respect. Some kind of respect will naturally come about. If I just look at you and say, "Hey, John...," then that respect really isn't there; it's not the same. So respect is instilled through the use of relative terms, and when that system based on the origin story is in place, then it's not difficult to understand that the sun and the moon are relatives. The wind is a relative because it's part of creation. So you talk to the wind. That tree is a relative. The water. Everything around you is a relative. But that's how you grew up, so you understand it.

When we were kids, every time I would go out to play, Mom would always say, "Don't forget, before you take a drink, say, 'Ṫuŋkaśila, Uŋśimalayo.'" Ṫuŋkaśila is a term of respect of a relative. Uŋśimalayo means "help me." So if I lie down to drink from the creek, I'll say, "Ṫuŋkaśila, Uŋśimalayo" (feminine would be Uŋśimalaye), asking that creek, that water, to address my thirst. I'm not asking that creek to pity me or have mercy on me but to help me with a need.[1] I am asking a relative to give me that water to give me strength and the ability to go on.[2]

As a Lakota child you grow up doing these things—addressing each creation as relatives. Because we're human, however, to stay focused on that way of living, there has to be something, some practice, to keep you focused, and that's how many of our ceremonies developed.

We don't worship a higher power. There is not a Supreme Being above us as there is in the Christian church. The spirit(s) that come into our ceremonies, it's the same as if you came to visit me. If you did that, we would sit and talk and share, and I do the same thing with that spirit. He comes in as a relative. He didn't come in to

1. Today the church has translated Uŋśimalayo to mean "have pity on me" or "have mercy on me." This word comes from uŋmaśike, which means "I have a need, but I know what that need is, so I will come to you and say 'Uŋśimalayo'— help me with this need and I will offer something in return." The church took those words and translated unmasike as "I'm pitiful; I'm helpless," so today Uŋśimalayo means "have mercy on me; have pity on me."

2. There are Wiwila Wiċaśa, water men. They are little men who live in the water, especially in or near springs. We talk to them when we take a drink from these waters.

control my life. He came in to say, "What do you need? How can I help?" And you tell him. You say, "Here's my need, and this is what I will do in return." And we're very fortunate because all they want from us are tobacco ties and flags, and that's what we give. Sometimes we go beyond that, and we offer ourselves by fasting on the hill and giving thanks for help with whatever needs we have expressed. We fast on the hill and give thanks to them for their help. We do that fast anywhere from one to four days. We call that fast the *haŋbleċeya*, or these days some people call it the vision quest. Vision quest, which is the English term, is very misleading because people think you go on the hill to seek a vision. But it's not for that. You spend your time on the hill because you have a specific need or you want to show appreciation for a special gift. There's a reason you do it, and before you go on that hill, you must be clear about that reason. Otherwise, you won't last. The *haŋbleċeya* is a challenging ceremony.[3]

Or we sun dance. The sun dance (and the vision quest) are both four-year commitments, so when you finish your four years, you've done your part. You might tell the spirit, "I'll do this for four years," and then when you're done, you're done. In return for their help, you might offer your body on the hill or in the sun dance because they always said the only possession we have is our body. In the sun dance we offer our body by piercing to the tree. When a sun dancer pierces, the moment he bleeds, he gives life back to creation; just as Inyaŋ bled for creation, so does a sun dancer. Women do flesh offerings. They don't pierce, but they do make flesh offerings. This is done by taking a piece of flesh, about the size of a bead on a moccasin, as an offering. Sometimes it might be one flesh offering, other times five or six. I don't know what the significance of numbers is in this case, as sometimes people do many flesh offerings.

Remember, the *tiośpayes'* focus is always on Miṫakuye Oyas'iŋ, "all my relatives." Regardless of what kind of personality you have,

3. *Haŋ* is short for *Haŋhepi*, or "nighttime." *Ble* means "I'm going on, or I am on, a journey." *Ċeya* could mean "crying" or "lamenting" or "appealing," and when we *haŋbleċeya*, we do this by speaking or singing. Sometimes we do cry up there; it all depends on our reason for doing it.

what influence you have, "all my relatives" remains the focus. We still see that today. The loyalty in each *tiošpaye* is still very strong. And some of the *tiošpayes* really have a hard time. They struggle. The behavior in them is not perfect, but they're intact, there's loyalty, and they work with Miťakuye Oyas'iŋ. So while we may sponsor a ceremony to ask for health or some other kind of help, they were developed mainly to stay focused on Miťakuye Oyas'iŋ. That's their true purpose.

Also, our ceremonies are there to help us when we weaken—physically or mentally. When we weaken, we go to these ceremonies to regain our physical and mental strength. When you go into the Inipi, you might not be able to finish the ceremony and come out early, but it doesn't mean you've failed. You look at yourself and say, "Why did I come out? Is it physical or mental?" Whatever that weakness is, you'll identify it and work on it, so the next time you go in, you'll be able to address it. The Inipi is where you find yourself physically, you find where you are mentally, and most important you begin to find out who you are. You will find yourself because in that ceremony, you will get a good look at yourself.

When you fast on the hill, you have to address those things as well. Sometimes it's a very scary situation because it comes from you. It doesn't come from out there. It comes out of you, and sometimes you have to make a decision, a little decision that's going to change your whole life. And that's where the scary part comes in.

A spirit will never tell you what to do.[4] A medicine man will never tell you what to do. They will make suggestions, you think about them, and you make the decision. They will tell you what the situation is and what can be done, and then you decide if you're going to do it. When they give you medicine, and it comes into your body, in most cases it opens up the antibiodies you already have within your system and lets your own body fight that disease. So their medicine, in most cases, doesn't do the curing; it just opens up the antibiodies

4. This is in the area of telling you to do ceremonies, or to carry a pipe, areas where a deep personal commitment is needed. In other areas, telling you to shape up or to quit drinking, they might tell you to do that.

in your immune system, and you fight your own disease. That can happen because all of us are born with everything we need, but there are times we need extra help in certain areas. And sometimes, similar to what happens in surgery, they'll take whatever the problem is out of you through ceremony. And that's also from their medicine. You might have gallstones, and their medicine will break it up into powder and you'll pass it. Instead of surgery, you'll pass it through because their medicine will break it up.

One medicine man I used to work with was a Heyoka.[5] In his ceremonies lightning would come in, enter the body, and burn out the disease or the problem. That lightning would burn out the disease that was there. I always tell people we have the real laser surgery.

Although we have ceremonies to address every need, just sponsoring one or going to one isn't enough. Each one of us has to take responsibility for our life. The responsibility for dealing with a problem always comes back to you. The problem and the options for receiving help always come back to you, and you decide if you are going to apply them or not.

There are two things that hold back our healing process most of all. The first is not taking responsibility, and the second is our lack of faith. Many of us have a difficult time having faith in our ceremonies because for so long we were told these ways were evil, that they were devil worship. I'm seventy, and people my age and older, we've been through the mill. We were whipped into believing that these ways were evil and, consequently, never taught them to our children and grandchildren. We did this in order to protect them from the abuse we suffered. Some of us eventually saw the value of our traditional ways and went back to them. Now we're slowly bringing them back. Our medicine men said they didn't want our people to be fooled by stories told against our ceremonies.

In all of our ceremonies it's important to remember Mitakuye Oyas'in, to remember that we are all relatives. That's how we address

5. The Heyoka is the contrary. The Heyoka is contrary to everything we consider normal behavior and speech. Whatever is positive to him is negative to us, and vice versa. The Heyoka spirit is from the Wakiyan Oyate, the Thunder nation.

them when we pray, as relatives. And we call them Ṫuŋḳaśila. Ṫuŋḳaśila. I would address them all as Ṫuŋḳaśila. All of them. All Miṫakuyeṗi—are my relatives. They are relatives, and we speak directly to them. The only exception to this is when I talk to the Thunder nation, the Wakiyan. Then I usually ask the eagle or the coyote to translate my prayers because I might make a mistake. If you are praying for health, the Wakiyan will hear sickness. I've heard people try to pray like a Heyoḳa, and they make a mistake because they don't really think like one. So I ask another nation to translate my prayers to the Wakiyan. They are still relatives; I just don't address them directly. The main thing, however, is they are all relatives.[6] If you want to talk to one in particular, you are still addressing a relative, the same as you might address an uncle or a friend who you know might be able to help.

If you're on the hill and a deer comes up to you, or an elk or an eagle, all that means is they are telling you they're listening. They aren't coming to give you a gift to become a medicine man. A lot of people see these things and they say, "That must be my spiritual guide, so I'm going to do ceremonies." They kind of create their own interpretation. They want to be that (medicine man) so bad that they look for anything to address them and give them a gift—you know, to get that position.

People seeking to become medicine men are a little like the early researchers who came here to the reservations with a theory. Historically, this has been a big problem. I mean, any one of us, when we want to research something, we come up with some theory and tend to think that's what we're going to confirm through our research. So we ask questions to confirm what we're thinking. You know, we all have experience with this in some way. We say, "Oh, yeah, I know what that means. I understand that," about whatever it is we're researching. So all researchers kind of have their own preconceived notions, and whatever they hear often leads toward that notion. And

6. You can address them as Ṫuŋḳaśila, or as Ṫuŋḳaŋ Oyaṫe (the group that represents the beginning of time until today, the Stone nation), or as Miṫakuyeṗi (my relatives).

when you tell them the real truth, they just kind of ignore it and say, "No, what I think is...," all the while trying to prove their theories.

So we're always having to clear up misconceptions about our culture and especially about our ceremonies. Even as recently as the 1950s and '60s, we were still very much in the grip of acculturation and assimilation. Our ceremonies were still illegal, and the church was very strong. Our ceremonies are no longer outlawed, and even though the effects of acculturation are still strong today, things are changing.

When we started the movement to bring back our spiritual ways in the 1960s, 1968 and '69, I didn't think I would see a change in my lifetime, but I saw it happen really fast. Today our ceremonies are in the open, and they are very strong. They're very important. It doesn't matter what culture you're from—our ceremonies really have an impact on everybody who participates in them.

*chapter nine*

# THE BUFFALO CALF PIPE
•
# PT̄E HIŋC̄ALA ĊAŋNUP̄A

Pte Hiŋc̄ala Ċaŋnup̄a, the Buffalo Calf Pipe: I want to share some stories about *ċaŋnup̄a*, the pipe. The pipe that individuals have is made out of hardwood for the stem and pipestone, from a quarry in Minnesota, for the bowl. These two items represent a connection to the spirit world and to all creation in the universe. The bowl and stem, when you put them together, create a means to connect to all creation.

There are different stories you'll hear about the pipe, and I want you to think about them. What is at the core of each story—where do they connect? This is often how we learn; we hear one story and then later another story, and somehow they connect and teach us something. It might even be hearing the same story again but told a little differently. Think about these stories in relationship to each other. In some of these stories there are individuals who either told me the story or have a role in it. Out of respect I will not mention them by name.

These days probably the most common story about the pipe is from the book *Black Elk Speaks.* Black Elk told of two scouts who went out from camp and after traveling a while saw an object approaching. As it came closer they saw a beautiful woman carrying a bundle. One began to have strong sexual desires for her and said, "She's alone, there's nobody around, let's have her," but the other scout said, "No, there's something special about her. Don't think about that." The one with desires insisted, and the woman approached and said, "One of you wishes to do something. So come." The scout went toward her and reached out, and a cloud enveloped them for a time. When it cleared the woman was still there, and a pile of bones from the scout lay before her. She told the other man to go back to his camp and tell the people to prepare a place for her. He rushed back and told the leader, and they built a huge lodge for this woman, who approached the camp singing a song. She came into the lodge and made four circles and presented the pipe to the leader of the camp, saying, "Respect and honor this pipe, and the people will live and multiply." She gave instructions for the care of the pipe and turned to leave. As she walked away she lay down and turned into a buffalo calf. The calf walked on and lay down, turning into a young buffalo. Arising and walking off, the young buffalo lay down, turning into a fully grown buffalo, and then, the fourth time, the grown buffalo lay down and got up as a white buffalo, walking away out of sight.

That's a general but pretty standard telling of the story that was written in *Black Elk Speaks.* When I read that story, I felt that it gave an image of rolling out the red carpet to receive someone very holy, someone surrounded by a glowing light. To me that story sounds like a description of the Blessed Virgin Mary or some Christ-like figure coming down to earth. That was my impression, and it made me think of someone to bow or kneel down to. That's the most common pipe-origin story out there today.

We have a lineage of guardians for the Pte Hiŋčala Ċaŋnuṗa. This next story comes from one of these guardians, who told it to me in the mid-1970s. This man died in 1998, but before that I would take my students to visit him, and he would come down to Rosebud from time to time. Once he came down to speak to a group of us, and we recorded him. I asked if I could use his stories, and he gave me permission to do so. This next story came to me from that man.

He said that a long time ago our people lived in the area of Bismarck, North Dakota, in that general area on both sides of the Missouri River. Every spring a relative from the Cheyenne nation would come to spend the summer with them and would return to his people in the fall. One fall, on his return journey, as he approached Devil's Tower, he noticed an opening on the east side.[1] This man had some spiritual gifts and knew there was something special about this opening, so he went to it and walked inside. It was an opening to a tunnel, and he walked for a while and came upon two objects, a bundle of arrows and a pipe. He spent some time looking at them and then took the bundle of arrows and continued down the tunnel, eventually emerging from Devil's Tower on the west side. Continuing on his journey, he walked on, though he turned back once and saw that the opening on the west side had closed. The opening in the side of Devil's Tower was no longer there. He took that bundle of arrows to his people, and they became the seven sacred arrows of the Cheyenne.

The following spring when he made his journey to the east, he found a great deal of excitement among our people. They told him that a woman had brought a gift. They told him the story of the two scouts—and here my friend's account of this event differs somewhat from Black Elk's. The two scouts had been out and met the woman, though when the man with sexual desires approached her and was enveloped in a fog, his friend became frightened and ran away. After running some distance, he felt ashamed that he had deserted his friend, that he had left him in a time of danger, and so he turned

1. Today it is a national monument in northeastern Wyoming. It is also called Bear's Lodge. One man told me it was once called Pté San He, White Buffalo Horn or Gray Buffalo Horn.

around and went back, finding only the bones of his companion. This man began to wander around in a state of confusion, eventually returning to the camp to tell what had happened. After he told his story, the leader of the camp told him, "That woman who frightened you brought a pipe." This woman had come to the camp before the scout returned, and she came as a normal woman, not to awe people but to bring a gift. My friend also said that when the woman turned to leave the camp, she changed four times into Wamakaṡkan, which means "a living being of the earth." He didn't say a buffalo. He said Wamakaṡkan. It could have been a horse, an elk, a deer, or a buffalo. He didn't specify, just that the woman had brought the pipe and on her departure turned into Wamakaṡkan.[2]

2. To me it's important that he didn't specify just one nation, the Buffalo nation. He said Wamakaṡkan, "all of creation," reinforcing our relationship with all of creation rather than one nation.

On hearing this story, the Cheyenne man asked to see the pipe, and when it was brought out he saw that it was the pipe he'd seen inside of Devil's Tower. He told the people his story of entering Devil's Tower and finding the objects inside and told them, "I left that pipe there." That is the version of this story told by a guardian of our pipe, and I believe it's an older story than Black Elk's.

One of my older brothers, who died several years ago, spent a great deal of time with our grandparents. He learned many stories from them, and one he shared with me concerned a time long ago when a group from the Cree Nation attacked a Lakota camp at dawn. They tried to kill everybody, but one woman survived. She was just knocked out, but they left her for dead along with the others, and when she woke up, she saw the entire camp had been wiped out. Then she heard a baby crying really hard, and she began to look around for it, only to find a buffalo calf walking through the camp crying like a baby. She took the calf and nursed it, and the calf stopped crying. After a while she decided to set out and look for other *tioṡpayes*. Just as she started out, she heard a voice that said, "You saved my son, and I will bring you a gift." When she turned to see who was speaking, she saw a huge bull buffalo standing on the ridge behind her. I believe this is one of the oldest stories I have heard about the origin of the pipe. It's a very old story.

Each of these stories tells of the pipe coming to us. We have another story about the time just after that event. When news of the pipe got out to the rest of our people, they had to make a decision about whether to accept it. In one of the largest *tiośpayes*, the camp leader had a Tiṗi put up and called the wisest members of his *tiośpaye* together. He told them to go inside and stay until they had reached a decision about accepting the pipe. The discussion lasted a long time, but eventually the wisest one came out and said a decision had been reached, but before announcing it there was something else to say. He said, "As far back as we can remember, we have fed the spirits of the deceased, and they help us. Every time I have a need, I feed the spirits of the deceased, and they help. We're going to keep that tradition." Then he said, "We have decided the pipe is a wonderful gift, a powerful gift, but if we're not careful, down the road we're going to step on each other and kill each other. We have decided to keep the pipe, but we are also going to keep that other way."

We call the practice of feeding the spirits Wagluhtatapi. Anytime you have a feast after a ceremony or a good meal, you take a small portion and offer it to the spirits. Mostly, these are spirits of deceased relatives. They say that many people have died and had no ceremonies done for them, so they are still roaming the earth. They say there are many of these spirits and they are hungry, so we feed them and in return they help us. They ensure that we will never starve. Whenever we have a gathering, a pow wow, or a feast, the first thing we do is offer food to the spirits.

The man who told me this story must have known what I was going to ask him because he said, "Well, I'll tell you how we got this practice of feeding the spirits." He then told me a story about the origin of Wagluhtatapi. He said that one night a woman was roasting some meat over the hot coals of her fire. Someone walked up outside her Tip̄i and asked to come in. The woman said yes, and a woman stepped into the lodge. She was alone, and the woman in the Tip̄i told her to sit. When she sat down she said, "Your cooking smelled so good, I came over." The host said, "Yes, and I have plenty." When the meat was done, she cut a piece of it and then some fat, put it on some leaves, and handed it to her. The visitor said, "If you have some extra, I'd like to ask for it because my father and my son are starving." The woman said of course, that she had plenty, so when the visitor was done eating, she prepared two servings and gave them to her to take back to her father and her son. As the visitor left the Tip̄i, she stopped at the door and said, "Tomorrow morning, tell your hunters to go over the hill behind your camp. Over that hill is a valley. Tell them to follow that valley, and they will come to this nation, this Oyaṫe, who will be waiting. Tell your people you must remember us. Tell them to take what they need and remember us." After the visitor had gone, the woman went to the leader of the camp and told him what had taken place. Then the leader called all the hunters together, told them the story, and said, "We must follow this direction."

At dawn the next day the hunters followed the directions given by the woman visitor, and when they came to the head of the valley, a herd of buffalo was standing there waiting for them. They killed what they needed, and when the meat had been butchered, the leader took the choicest cut and cooked it. Then he selected one of his hunters and said, "Take this meat to the top of a hill and offer it to them." The man took the meat up the hill and asked the spirits to recognize the gift and to accept it. He said, "May you never starve in your world, and may you help us that we will never starve in ours." So that's where Wagluhṫaṫapi, feeding the spirits, comes from. That's what it means. That's why today, when we have ceremonies, we pray with the pipe, but when we're going to eat, we offer food to the spirits.

Pretty recently, about fifteen years ago, I stopped in on a summer afternoon to visit a local medicine man, who was home by himself. He said, "I had some interesting visitors this morning." I asked who they were, and he said, "This morning I heard someone knocking on the door, so I went and opened it. There was an old man and a young man standing there, and I had never seen these people. I asked them to come in, and they did and sat down on the couch." He said, "I went into the kitchen to heat up the coffee, and the old man said, 'We've just come to tell you something. We are starving. We must go.'" My friend said, "I turned around and saw them get up and go outside, so I turned off the stove and went out to see them off, and there was nobody around. It was still early, but the sun was up and it was full daylight. I walked around the house, looked all over, and there was nobody." Shortly after he told me this story, we had some ceremonies, and they said there are many spirits on this earth that are still roaming around, and they are starving not just for food, but for prayers.

When we learned this information, people began to come and put on ceremonies. That year some students at the university were talking about some of the problems on the reservation, particularly alcoholism. They wanted to do something about it and wondered what they could do to bring that issue into the open. After we talked about it, we decided to do a walk. I was at the meeting and told them the story you just read. We decided to walk from Kilgore to St. Francis and to stop and pray at every place where somebody had been killed in a car wreck on that stretch of road.[3] Nearly all the deaths on that road were alcohol related. Sometimes the people who died were sober, but drunk drivers ran into them. We decided to do the walk on April 21, and a bus was to take us to Kilgore at six in the morning. When I woke that morning the day of the walk, it was snowing hard. It was a ground blizzard. My wife asked me what I thought about making the walk that day, and I decided to go to our meeting place

3. Kilgore, Nebraska, is a small town about twenty miles south of St. Francis, just off the reservation. It's a popular place to buy alcohol.

and see if anyone showed up. When I got there people were already arriving, and we took the bus to Kilgore and stopped to pray in front of the bar in that town. Then we started to walk to St. Francis, and I never realized how many deaths had taken place on that road. It was really interesting, because we all began to feel better that something was being done for those who had died there. Now a walk happens every year. I think the following year they walked from White River to Mission. Each year they select a stretch of road to walk, stopping along the way to pray for the dead, and it's because some spirits brought that need to our attention.

So there are different ways that Lakota people express their needs or give thanks. One way is with the pipe; another is in feeding the spirits. We say the pipe is for health, for health and growth. The pipe can help you live a good life; it's like a relative standing by you all the time who will help you when you're weak and need to correct your-self.[4] Keep in mind, however, that the pipe, the čaŋnupa, is Wakaŋ. *Wa* is one of the creations that has *kan*, and *kan* refers to a being with the power to give or take life, the power to build or destroy. Good and bad are within the čaŋnupa in equal proportions, so you must be careful with it. There are enormous responsibilities that come with carrying the pipe, so you never tell anybody that they should carry one: even the spirits won't tell you to carry the pipe. The responsibilities that come with the pipe are to live a good life, a life of honor, respect, and love. A life that embodies the idea of Mitakuye Oyas'iŋ.

4. The pipe as a relative is the traditional Lakota relationship. Today, we've been so conditioned to Western thinking that this relationship has been distorted, and the pipe is often raised above us, like an altar to be worshiped. This concept came from the church.

*chapter ten*

## CARE AND USE OF THE PIPE
### •
### ĊAŋNUP̄A GLUONIHAŋ UŋP̄I

As I mentioned in the last chapter, in our tradition we have a person who keeps the P̄te Hiŋċala Ċaŋnup̄a, the original pipe. There is a lineage of guardians, or keepers, and the current keeper is the nineteenth in this lineage. That figure could be misleading to some people, because today we count one generation as something like twenty-five years. That's the time of one generation using today's Western measurement. Lakota measurement, however, is different. Red Cloud described our measurement of a generation in his negotiations with the federal government over the Black Hills, when he said, "If we agree on this, I will be the first generation until the day I die. My son will be the next until the day he dies, then my grandson. It will go like that." So by our measurement a man can live for three or four generations according to Western thought, and when the current man says he's the nineteenth-generation keeper of the pipe, it's kind of hard to understand just how long it's been since the first one. Oral tradition acknowledges him as the nineteenth-generation official keeper of our pipe. Oral tradition says the pipe is somewhere around twenty-five hundred years old.

Our pipe keepers have a big responsibility, and it is a challenging position. Like anyone in a position of big responsibility, they receive a lot of criticism. Also, people supposedly have dreams or visions that they are to take the pipe or do something with it, and our keepers have to deal with that. It's very hard being the official keeper of the Pte Hiŋċala Ċaŋnupa.

Once again, to carry a pipe is each individual's choice. The pipe brings out who you really are, and sometimes in that process you have to make some changes in order to live a good life. They say the minute you decide to keep a pipe, you start to prepare for it to come into your life. When you receive a pipe you should have a Ċaŋtojuha, a pipe bag.[1] Originally, this term was *Ċaŋte ojuha*. Today it has been shortened to *Ċaŋtojuha*, and it means a covering for the heart. Today we simply call it a pipe bag, but you must prepare that cover for that heart. A pipe becomes your heart. You must never keep the pieces connected. The moment you put the bowl and stem together, it becomes an instrument that brings about whatever you say or think.

Some years ago we used to load a pipe and place it in our lodge before we went in for a sweat ceremony. A medicine man came to our sweat one time and told us to wait until we were in the lodge and prepared to begin the ceremony before we loaded the pipe.[2] He said, "That pipe is in the lodge loaded, and all of you are still outside joking and telling stories, saying things that you wouldn't want to come true. Never load that pipe until you start the ceremony." So the pipe is the instrument we use to make connections to creation. The pipe opens that channel for us to make a connection to any creation on earth or anywhere in the universe. The communication is very strong.

Sometimes I share stories with a woman over on Pine Ridge, and once she told me she had just heard something about the pipe that

1. *Ojuha* is a "container" or "cover," and *Ċaŋte* is "heart."

2. To load the pipe you offer a pinch of tobacco to each direction, including above and the earth, and a seventh pinch from you, for your part in it, for your need or appreciation. Each pinch is put into the bowl of the pipe after it is offered. Then a rolled-up ball of sage is placed to cap the top and keep other thoughts from entering your prayers.

she'd never heard anyone speak of before. She said there was an elderly man living near her and that she visited him often to hear his stories. He told her there was something he wanted to share with her, something about the pipe that he never heard people discussing. He said, "Before the pipe came to us we were Ikčé Wičaśa. When that pipe came to our people, they talked it over, and the ones that decided to accept that pipe became Lakota, Dakota, or Nakota. The others remained Ikčé Wičaśa. If you pick up the pipe, you become Lakota. If not, you are Ikčé Wičaśa, an ordinary man or ordinary being." He said, "Lakota is an expression of addressing a relative. If I address you as a Lakota, then I'm saying that you are my relative in that road of praying with the pipe." I've asked around myself and asked my students to ask people about that story. It's an interesting story, and we do know that *Lakota* is not just a name; it means more than that. It means acknowledging a relative. *Lakota* does not mean you are an Indian. It means you have accepted a way of peace and harmony within yourself and with all creation and you walk that road.

Today you hear someone say they are a pipe carrier. I think that's a New Age term, because when I ask our elders about it, they all say they've never heard of that expression. If you have a pipe, it's yours alone, and you keep it, and you use it when you need to. You don't do ceremonies with it unless you are called upon to do so, and then you can share your pipe. You don't carry it around. You keep it in a safe place. A man who lives near me was telling me that one time, his house was filled up with stuff. He said the way we live today, we just accumulate more and more stuff, more junk. So his house was so full he didn't know where to keep his pipe. He had a small shed out back where he thought it would be safe, so he put it out there. Right after that, every night, someone would be knocking at the door. He'd go to see who it was, and there would be nobody around. He couldn't figure it out, but after three or four nights, he decided to bring the pipe back into the house, and after that there was no more knocking. It didn't want to stay out there in the shed.

The pipe has these abilities. That's why they say it's dangerous, but it's important to know that the danger is really us. We are the danger. When we hold that pipe and pray with it, if we're angry or hateful, those things will come out. The pipe didn't cause them; we did. That's why they all say it's dangerous. They all say to be careful. The pipe will bring out your true feelings and show who you really are.

Just remember, the pipe is an instrument. It's an instrument that helps you make a clear connection to creation. It's not that you are not connected all the time; the pipe just helps you make that connection clearer and stronger. It's just an instrument, and if you have a pipe, then whenever you have a need, you get by yourself and smoke it. You don't perform pipe ceremonies just because you have a pipe. We have people who are designated to do that in our ceremonies. If a friend or a group comes to you and asks that you load your pipe and pray with them, then you can do it to honor their request. You don't have to be a medicine man or woman to do that, but you do it only on request.

There are four situations we're particularly careful of with the pipe. If a woman is on her moon, she should not pray with the pipe or be present when others are doing so. If she removes herself from a pipe ceremony with respect, she gets just as much help as if she smoked it because she respects herself and she respects the pipe. There shouldn't be any animals or other pets present when praying with the pipe. Abusive language should not be used around the pipe, and no one under the influence of alcohol or drugs should be present. There is one other concern as well, and it's pretty touchy to bring up, but if a person has the blood of their people on their hands, they should never hold the pipe. In other words, if you murder one of your own people, you can never hold that pipe. When veterans come back from war, there are ceremonies to cleanse them, but even then some of them say they don't want to carry a pipe because of having taken a human life. By not taking the pipe, a veteran will get just as much help in showing that respect. They say that when warriors came back from fighting (or young men returned from a *zuya*), they would stop a distance from camp, and any who had taken human life would have their face painted black. Relatives of these men would come out from the camp and take them into a sweat lodge to wipe that death off them before they would be allowed to enter the camp. Under those circumstances, however, they said it was all right for these warriors to hold the pipe after the cleansing because the human life they took was in defense of their people. If they had murdered one of their own people, they would not be allowed to hold the pipe. This prohibition is still being debated today among some of our people, and some of them get upset when the subject is brought up.

So we have a lot to learn about these ways, a lot to understand, and we can't just talk about it and think about it. We have to do it. Taking action always involves some risk, but that's what we have to do. Our pipe keepers talk about people visiting them and asking when they should get a pipe. They said they would always tell these people to get one when they were ready, and usually the next question would be, "How do I know when I'm ready?" The only answer to that is that you should know when you are ready, and sometimes you know only by taking up the pipe and learning and growing with it. There is no designated time when you should or shouldn't take it up. If you are sincere, it will teach you.

Also, they say the pipe will take care of itself. If you use it properly, it will take care of you as well. It's a wonderful gift. The only thing to be afraid of is yourself. When you hold that pipe, you should be aware of what you are thinking and what you are praying for.

Every pipe is different, depending on its owner. Each one has its owner's symbols and designs on it. Again, no one can tell somebody to hold or carry the pipe. I've been told that even the spirits can't tell you to do this. It's a personal decision, and once you pick it up, you are picking up a way of life. So you need to understand what that way of life is, and one of the main ways of learning this is in doing it. It's impossible to understand everything ahead of time, so we usually have to jump in and learn by experience.

Also, it's important to understand that when you make a mistake using the pipe, it is simply a mistake. You learn from it and go on. Today some of us are so conditioned to good and evil and the concept of sin that when we make a mistake, we immediately think of punishment. We think something bad is going to happen. Well, if you ask them just what is going to happen, they say they don't know but something bad is coming. In our way, though, it's just a mistake, and you learn from it and try not to do it again. The Lakota philosophy is very open about these things. We know that people make mistakes, but the church has taught us that if you make a mistake, you commit a sin. You feel very guilty and know you will be punished. This idea of guilt has been so driven into us that we're all afraid. We should all be free to experience and learn; that's how we grow.

When we pray with the pipe, and in our ceremonies as well, we burn sweetgrass (Waċaŋġa) and sage (Ṗeji Hoṫa). The aroma of sweetgrass is sweet and mellow. It draws spiritual energy, but you have to remember that it draws both the good and the bad. That sweet aroma will draw both, so we burn the sage to repel the negative. And again, the negative we're trying to repel is the negative within us. If we think positively, we draw the positive, and if we think, feel, or act negatively, we draw that energy. Many people think that there is energy out there that makes us good or bad, but it's actually up to us. It's our responsibility. In working with the pipe, that's something you learn.

They always say that the most difficult thing in life is to make a decision. Until that point, there seem to be many possibilities, but when we make a decision, we have to stick with that one way. So, finally, we make a decision, a choice in life, and we use our ceremonies to help. In this case, we use the pipe ceremony to help with our decision. We use the pipe to bring us together as relatives. One meaning of ceremony, as I understand it, is that we come together as one, and there are certain things we must all observe in all our ceremonies. First of all, we need to examine ourselves and analyze our motivation. The cautions I mentioned earlier should be honored. Then the environment should be positive; we need to smudge ourselves and come together in a positive mood. This is all because the moment that pipe stem and bowl are joined together, whatever you are thinking or saying will come true. Putting the pipe together will make the connection that will send your thoughts and words to all of creation, and somebody out there might make them happen. The pipe has that power. We use it to communicate with all creation.

So the pipe is a channel of communication we use to talk to our relatives; the tree, the eagle, the coyote, the air, the sun—we talk to them as relatives. We talk to them and say, "Here's what I'm going to do about my need." You know, if I have a problem, I might talk to a number of people. I'll get advice from them and then think about it and make a decision about what I'm going to do about that problem. It's the same way with the pipe: I load my pipe, and I tell creation what I am going to do about my problem. I tell them what I am going to do and ask for help in that process. I tell them if they can help, that would be good, and if not, then that's fine as well, but at least be aware of what I am doing. The pipe will send that message to all creation, and one medicine man said the smoke will carry that message, and somebody along the way will see it and shoot it down and will help you.[3] That's kind of a dramatic image, but these men sometimes use examples like that. So, today you often hear the term *pipe ceremony*, and this is what it means, that you use the pipe to bring everything together as one and communicate your needs. I hope you don't

3. "Somebody" in this instance means any relative, any living being or spirit in all creation. The help is there in the physical or spiritual world, so when your request reaches the one who can help, they will respond.

have the idea that the pipe is unapproachable or dangerous. It's a wonderful gift.

Earlier I mentioned that some of our stories might require a little thought in order to understand their message. One of these stories from my own life is the time I arrived at my home on Rosebud in the early evening. It was some years ago, and there weren't any other houses around it like there are today, just my house and a lot of space all around. When I got home, I saw that the whole area in back of my house was covered by a flock of birds. I looked up and saw what looked like a huge cloud in the sky, and it was more birds. I said, "That's the biggest flock of birds I've ever seen." My brother-in-law was with me at the time, and he said, "Take a closer look." I looked again and saw that they were all hawks. Every bird out there was a hawk. Different kinds and shapes and sizes, but they were all hawks. I mentioned this to a man I used to sing with—he and I would sing for different medicine men—and he said, "Yes, I witnessed the gathering of the Owl nation one time. I never knew there were so many different owls." He said that the elders said that, periodically, every species in creation will do that; they will gather like that to renew the relationship among themselves. They will gather to renew and strengthen that relationship. He said, "We have the hardest time doing that. Humans have the hardest time gathering and uniting as relatives, and we are the most destructive species in creation because of that difficulty. We need to be able to do that."

So I began to understand more about Miṫakuye Oyas'iŋ, and how it works, when I witnessed that gathering. And I saw how it relates to the pipe and Wolakoṫa. As I've said, *Wolakoṫa* means "peace," and that is one of the goals in life when you carry the pipe; that's what it's for. A Lakota (also Dakota and Nakota) is a person of peace and harmony, most important within himself. The purpose of the pipe is for this, peace and unity. The pipe is for peace and health. It is to make that connection and harmony with all creation.

# chapter eleven

# THE SUN DANCE

•

# WIWAŋG WAĊIP̄I

Wiwaŋg Waċip̄i. Our sun dance has been held as far back as people can remember, though a long time ago it wasn't done like it is now. I think that's partly because of the ease of travel today. Today sun dances can be very large, but a long time ago people would sometimes dance alone. Either way, it's a way of giving thanks or asking help for a need. It's always done for a specific reason. I think that when it was done in smaller groups or even by individuals, it was probably done in slightly different ways than our large dances today.

When the missionaries came here and saw the dance and the piercing, they looked on it as self-mutilation. Of course, there is blood, but their view was a very negative way of looking at that ceremony. So they outlawed it (along with our other ceremonies) and called it a savage rite. It was in 1880 when our ceremonies were outlawed, and at that point our songs and practices went underground. After 1880 the sun dance was done privately and very quietly.

In the 1950s and '60s we were allowed to sun dance on the Pine Ridge Reservation, but they didn't allow anyone to pierce. So those who danced, they would dance and pray, but they weren't allowed to pierce. Then in 1968, when the movement to bring back our spirituality started, we brought back piercing as part of the sun dance. This was a real challenge at the time, and I think that most of our people were awed by it in the beginning. They wondered why it was being done, why dancers were piercing themselves. That practice had been outlawed for nearly one hundred years, and many of our people had forgotten the belief behind piercing. The whole idea, though, the belief behind it, is that the moment the sun dancer bleeds, he gives life back to creation. Just as Iŋyaŋ bled to create and give life, the sun dancer does the same.

The sun dance is a very physical challenge. It's a big commitment for anyone to make, and the commitment is to four years of dancing. Our sun dance songs are one of the ways we address that challenge. If you understand the songs, the wording, they will help you to have the energy you need to stay out there in the circle. There are times when the dancers weaken, but if you have a good group of singers, they'll notice when that happens, and they'll sing certain songs that bring energy back to the circle. One time it was really hot, and we were just barely able to move around, but the singers noticed and sang a fast song, a very fast one, and then when they finished that first song, they went into a slower one. But that first one brought that energy back; the words and the rhythm brought it back. They made us dance hard out in that hot weather, but they brought that energy back very quickly.

It's a beautiful ceremony, a beautiful dance. It's hard, and you've got to love the songs and the whole idea of dancing out there to survive. It's also a powerful ceremony, and it can really entice you. That's why I always caution people and tell them it will draw them in, but when that happens, don't come out and make a pledge to dance. If you do, then two weeks down the road, you're going to say, "What have I done?" You've got to understand what the dance is before you do it, and you've got to have a very good reason to do it. If you don't have that, you won't last. Dancers have to stay focused so that when they tire, they can focus on why they're dancing. That brings them back to why they're doing it. You have to pace yourself as well; it's a long four days. As a sun dancer, you learn to adjust to any situation, physically and mentally; you can adjust to any situation that comes up. So it teaches you a lot of things. It teaches you humility, and it teaches you about yourself and your own strength. It also teaches you about your weaknesses.

As I said, a sun dance can be done by any number of people. Today some of the dances are big, but there are also stories of individuals dancing alone. The sun dance is a personal commitment, and everyone chooses how they will do it. Whoever is running a dance does it according to their vision. If your vision is to dance alone, however, then that is how you will do it. When I started our dance, I had helped a medicine man run a dance for twelve years. I had decided to dance at Kyle, South Dakota with an adopted brother named John Around Him, but the medicine man that helped me said, "You live here. This is your home. You belong here." He said, "You dance here, and I'll help you. Even if it's just you, I'll help you." And that's how I started. I was prepared to dance by myself, but luckily I didn't have to. A lot of relatives came around and said, "We'll dance with you."

I hadn't planned any of it, but this medicine man invited me to some sweat ceremonies and later on showed me a piece of land and said, "You dance here." One of my relatives was also helping him at that time, and he heard us talking and said, "I'll dance with you." That's how our dance started, and that first year I practically built the whole thing myself—the whole shade arbor, all of it. My relative was working during the day, so in the evenings he'd come and help. During the day I was doing all of it. Then another relative came out to see me, and he said, "I heard you're gonna dance over there, so I'll help you." I went out to the dance grounds a few days later,

1. Wood supports for the dance arbor, usually made from small trees.

and found that he had cut all the crutches and stringers for me.[1] I couldn't believe it. I mean, he cut *all* of them and then hauled them out there. So the medicine man and I went out there and measured out the area we wanted to use, and I started.

I started work on the grounds in the last part of June, and back then this medicine man's uncle used to live with him. Every time I was out there working, his uncle used to come out there with a plastic milk jug filled with water, and he would sit there and smoke and visit while I worked. One day I was by the east gate of the arbor, standing there thinking, "Why am I doing this?" Nobody else was around, it was really hot, and I was really questioning myself, when he said, "Sit down. Have a smoke. Sit down. Take a break." So I sat down. I lit a cigarette, and he said, "Did you ever see me go in a sweat lodge?" And I said, "No, I haven't. I've seen you set it up and watch the fire and watch the door, but I've never seen you in there." He said, "I can tell you anything you want to know about the sweat lodge—anything. I can tell you anything about the sun dance that you want to know. Anything you want, I can tell you. The only reason I didn't participate in either one is because I can't do what you're doing now. Every sun dancer needs to do this. So they know they're part of the dance. They know their home." That man's words gave me so much energy. I couldn't believe how much it helped me to hear him say that, and after that it seemed like everything went fast. So sometimes a little encouraging word like that makes a big difference.

Today many dances are run by medicine men. I began to sun dance here on Rosebud at a dance run by a medicine man. I helped him for at least twelve years. Before that I used to help him with his altar and had known him for maybe twenty years. I helped him run a sun dance for twelve years. About halfway through that time, he asked me how I felt about white people dancing. I said, "Personally, I don't care who dances. I believe in this 'all my relatives' concept." He said he was thinking of letting some white men he knew dance with him. At that time it was a new idea, so I said, "This year when the dancers come, let's tell them our plan. Let's give them a year to think about it and tell them that next year when they come back, we'll make our decision. That way they'll have a year to either come back or go someplace else, but we'll give them a year to think about it."

He agreed with me, so that year at the sun dance we told them what we were thinking about and that the next year we were going to make a decision. We told them we wanted each one to pray about it. The following summer the majority of the dancers said they'd go along with whatever decision we made. Only a couple of them said they thought we shouldn't allow white people to dance. That medicine man said, "Well, we're going to do it, so you have one year to make up your mind to come back, or you can go someplace else." Then a year following that, all those dancers came back, but one of them was really upset, really mouthy out there in the circle. The first white man who danced with us was a friend of mine who lived on the reservation. We had to tell him that we couldn't defend him from criticism out there because we were going to catch just as much or more. We told him he was welcome to dance with us, but he had to stand on his own, and he agreed to that.

The first day of the dance that year, this one guy was just mouthing off, really criticizing my friend and all of us. Just this one guy. So finally, another helper and I took him in the sweat lodge, and I told him, "You know, a year ago we told you we were going to do this. So when you came back, I just assumed you were going to work with it." This man was from back east, and I told him, "If anybody should hate the white people, it's the medicine man and me because we were both born and raised here, and all our lives we've faced everything you're mouthing off about. We have decided to forgive, and that's what we're going to do. If you're uncomfortable with that, you make your own decision. If you're going to dance with us, pray about your prejudice, your anger. I know you, and I know you're not really prejudiced, but I know you're very angry. You have a lot of hatred in you, and I want you to deal with that." He sat there for a long time, and he said, "I want to take my pipe and go. I don't think I can forgive." I said, "That's your decision," and he got his pipe and left. He didn't dance with us again, but he kept coming back to the dance. I don't know if he ever danced again, but he kept coming back.

When this medicine man asked me to run the dance I started, I told him there were a couple of things I wanted to tell him and ask him about. I said I wouldn't be here today if somebody hadn't given me a hand, but somebody did, and that somebody wasn't just a Lakota. He was a white man, he was a black man, he was a Crow Indian, a Navajo, but when I was down, he gave me a hand. I said, "When I was four years old, my father died, and my mother died when I was sixteen. I pretty much raised myself, but I was able to recognize the people who helped me. Some Mexicans gave me help when I was way down, and I want to give something back." I said, "I don't care who comes through that gate; if they come sincerely, I'll let them dance with me because I believe they're my relatives."[2] The medicine man said, "I'm glad to hear that because I have adopted some white people. They brought their son to me, and my spirits healed him, and they want to give thanks through the sun dance. I took them around the reservation, and nobody will accept them in their dance. It really hurts me and makes me sad, because at a few of these dances, when they saw me with these people, they asked me to leave too." And this medicine man was a sun dancer; he'd run sun dances himself. He said, "I'm glad to hear your decision. I'll bring them here." I did ask him to let me talk to them first, not because they were white but to have an idea if they were really ready to dance. He said he'd go along with that request.

After we had that talk, he said, "So what's the other thing you want to talk about?" I told him I didn't want a medicine man to run

2. There is a gate in each of the four directions. Dancers enter in the morning and leave at the end of the day through the east gate.

the dance. I told him I had equal respect for each of our medicine men. I said, "I've known you guys for over twenty years. I sang for some of you guys, helped a lot of you. I've translated for many of you, and I have a lot of respect for you, but frankly, I don't trust your followers. If you or another medicine man runs this dance, the dancers are not going to focus on the sun dance; they're going to focus on you and look to you for every little thing that comes up. They're going to depend on you for answers, just like they depend on priests and ministers. They're going to come running to you all the time and not take responsibility as dancers. I want this dance to be their ceremony and for them to know they're responsible for it. They're going to have to be responsible; otherwise, I won't let them dance." He said he agreed with me, that a long time ago medicine men never ran sun dances. He said that a sun dance is a people's ceremony, but that a medicine man would always be around in case somebody needed help. "But to be sure," he said, "let's bring another medicine man and ask him." So we brought another medicine man over, and we had

Sun dance altar •
Wiwaŋg waćiṗi owaŋka

a sweat ceremony, and he said he agreed and was happy to hear how we were going to do it. He said, "I'll support you." So we decided that these two medicine men would have ceremonies to help me run the sun dance. In these ceremonies they told their spirits to be there to help me, and they said they would always be there with that help.

At a ceremony we had with some of these men, I asked them about something I'd seen at other dances, where the medicine man would have an altar in the back of the arbor, out of the circle. When I asked about that, one medicine man said that the sun dance itself is an altar. That's the altar. The only thing you need in that circle is your pipe. That's all you need because your altar is there. If there is another altar set up somewhere else, that belongs to that medicine man. That's the medicine man's altar, but it's not the sun dance, the sun dance altar. It's his altar sitting over there, and that means there are two different altars. He said a person could pray at one or the other.

I said that I was going to let the dancers bring their own medicine men to help them pierce, and they really liked that idea. I wanted to do it that way because at the last dance where I helped, one of my nephews danced for the first time, and when he was ready to pierce, he asked me if this medicine man he always went to could pierce him. I told him I had no problems with that, but we needed to ask the medicine man running the dance. When we asked that man he said no, that the other medicine man had to dance with him before that could happen. I told him that this other medicine man knew all about sun dances, that he was family, but he stuck to his decision and said he didn't want it to happen.

So when I told them about how I wanted to do it, the medicine men said it was a good idea. We agreed that if they wanted to do a ceremony, they could come into the circle and do it. That was our agreement. So I had those discussions with them before I started the dance, and that's how we started off.[3]

3. I am happy with how this has worked. One time we had nine medicine men in the circle, and all had come at the request of a dancer. When we notice one out there, we will bring him to the center and pray with the *čaŋnupa*. These men have a very difficult life, so we will pray with them and dedicate a round to help them. None of them has ever tried to tell me what to do out there.

I wanted to be clear before I started because I knew about that ceremony. I knew what the sun dance is and what it entails. I had my share of experience, and I needed to be very clear before I took responsibility in that way. Both of the medicine men I went into the lodge with agreed with me, so we went ahead and started the dance.

Many other dances are run by medicine men, but I'm not too familiar with how they're run. I don't try to understand them or see how they're doing things. It's their sun dance, and I respect that.

You know, the sun dance is something you don't take lightly; you have to be very clear about why you're doing it. You don't go into that dance and ask, "What can I do?" They always told me the sun dance is not a place to seek, or validate, a dream or vision. It's not a place to seek a gift or powers, to try to become a medicine man or woman. The sun dance is an annual gathering of all the powers on earth and in the universe. We call them all together, knowing that both negative and positive energies are present, and that's why we prepare for at least one year before that first year of dancing. We prepare to gain an understanding of ourselves and our reason for dancing. After that first year of dancing, it becomes a daily preparation for the next year. You live the life of a sun dancer, a life of Wolakota. You practice that so you will be prepared when you go into that circle with a need and to give thanks for the health and help you receive. You work with each other in that circle, and the songs help you to make that connection to the tree and to the relatives.[4]

The sun dance is a place of sacrifice. It's a four-day ceremony, and during those four days at some point, when a man is ready, he will pierce.[5] Sometimes this will be on one side of his chest, sometimes on both sides. He has a fifty- to sixty-foot rope, forked on one end, which will be attached to the pegs on his chest. He is pierced at the skin level, the peg is slipped under the skin, and the rope is attached. The other end of the rope is tied to the tree. At the appropriate time

4. Not having a medicine man to run the dance, the dancers become the ones performing the ceremony. We've witnessed a lot of healing and help among our dancers, and I think it's because they work together and take responsibility to perform this ceremony.

5. Traditionally, women did not pierce but made flesh offerings. Today, at some dances, women pierce, usually on the arm.

6. Years ago a knife was used for piercing. Today we use a scalpel.

the sun dancer will approach the tree four times, and on the fourth he will pull back and break from the tree. As I said, in the moment a sun dancer pierces and bleeds, he gives life back to creation.[6] Just as Iŋyaŋ bled to create and give life, the sun dancer does the same.

Years ago, only a few would sun dance because it was so difficult. It's a very difficult ceremony. At some dances everyone fasts, at others it's a personal choice, but all sun dancers abstain from drinking or touching water during the four days of the dance.[7] The sun dancer works with creation as a relative, from sunrise to the end of that day. He does not worship a Supreme Being. He says this is what I am giving in return for what I ask. I'd guess that around 80 percent of our sun dancers are in there because they are praying for a loved one, or a family, or maybe for the people. Maybe another 10 percent or 15 percent dance because they are seeking clarity, looking for identity, or a purpose, and then maybe 5 percent do it just to impress somebody, a boyfriend or girlfriend, or to get recognition. These 5 percent usually suffer the most. So we have many reasons for dancing. Every dancer has a personal reason to be out there, and that's between them and the relatives.

7. Many of us are not in good health, physically or psychologically. Sometimes the last choice we make for our health is to sun dance. Our medicine men understand this situation we're in today, so they allow diabetics and others with severe illnesses to eat and drink in the evening after the dance, but even these dancers abstain from water.

8. The vow, or commitment, to dance is for four years. The reason for this is that it takes time, but by the fourth year you will fully understand why you dance and, most important, yourself.

One young woman danced with us for four years. After she completed her vow, I didn't see her for a few years, and then I ran into her in Rapid City.[8] She told me that she had a story she wanted to share about her time at the dance. She said, "My mother dropped me off alone the first day of purification.[9] I had a tent and some bedding and some food, but I didn't know anyone there besides you and your family, and I didn't know you that well. I felt so lonely. I began to struggle with that feeling, and then when the dance started, it got worse. Every day at some point somebody would go to the mic and talk about their son or daughter, maybe their grandchild, some relative that was in the circle, and they would talk about them and offer support. I had no one to speak for me, and I felt so lonely, but then, on the third day, a man got up and said he was going to sing a song

9. There are four days of purification before the dance begins. We evaluate ourselves and gauge whether we're ready. We do the Inípi for these four days to help in this process.

for all the dancers. He began to sing, and the words to the song said, 'Look to the west, your relatives are there, talk to them. Look to the north, your relatives are there, talk to them.' By the time he got to the south, I just felt happy because I understood that I had relatives all around me. We all do." She said, "I never understood that phrase Miṯakuye Oyas'iŋ, 'all my relatives,' until that moment. When that man sang, I understood it clearly."

So every dancer has a different experience, and they are all very human experiences. Sun dancers are out there for four days in whatever weather comes to them. They feel this ceremony as a human being, and whatever they accomplish out there, they accomplish as a human being. It's a wonderful ceremony. I do it every year, and when I'm done, I know I'm ready for another year. Sometimes, in early spring, I question myself: am I really going to do it again? Last year one of my friends questioned it and pointed out that I was getting up in age. I had to laugh because he's right, but I told him that I've danced for more than twenty-five years, and every year I've questioned it in the spring. It's a challenging ceremony, and that's just the way it is, but when the time comes, I'm ready. I don't want to run a sun dance from the side, because I'm there to pray in the circle. I have prayers of my own, and my way of sacrificing, and that's why I participate. I'm not a leader out there. I go there and pray, and I welcome the others dancing with me. But I have to admit that every year, I ask that question.

*chapter twelve*

# OUR INIPI ORIGIN STORY AND PRACTICE

•

## OINI GLUIYESKAPI

*Inipi*. The word *ni* means "to be alive." *I* refers to whatever resource gives that life. When you go into the sweat lodge, *I* is that source which gives you life. *Pi* is just a plural form. So Inipi means "they are receiving life." You go into that lodge, really, to be born again, to be alive again. It's a physical and a mental cleansing. There are a lot of different descriptions or references to this. One is that it is like going back into your mother's womb, where you are cleansed and given life, and then you come out into the world fully refreshed and ready to meet life's challenges again.

We use the Inipi for many different things, but if you're perfect, you don't need it. We go in there because we have a need. There are many times I crawl in there because I'm angry, frustrated, lonely, jealous, sad over something, envious; it can be for anything that is bringing you down. You go in there, and you share with the Stone people—we call them people—when they come in.[1] You ask them for help and inspiration. The Water nation comes in to create that steam to cleanse your body, to open the pores and cleanse your body.

1. When the heated stones are brought into the lodge.

The heat and the steam are the medicine that comes to you, so you welcome them when you go in there. You make that connection to the Stone and the Water people and let them come to you to help you. At the same time, you let out whatever negative emotions or feelings you have, and they help you with that, and then when you come out, you are cleansed and refreshed. You might even be a little zapped because of the intensity of the ceremony itself. It can be a very intense little gathering in there.

In studying our language, I've been thinking about the meanings of our words, and sometimes I have a hard time calling activities like the Inipi ceremonies or rituals. To me, when I say "ceremony" or "ritual," it has a reference to some kind of religious system. I feel more comfortable calling activities like the Inipi celebrations. In the Inipi, for instance, I get together with relatives, human, stone, water, fire, and then we call on all the relatives around us. We call on them and celebrate our relationship, we celebrate togetherness, and we share our needs with each other.[2] When you celebrate like that, you are able to open up and relax, and that is the intent of the Inipi ceremony. It will help you to center yourself again, and other creations, like the spirit world, can more easily communicate with us when we are cleansed and open like that. We live in a world where there is a lot of negative energy; we live with it every day, and somehow we need to cleanse ourselves so we can connect with the spirits. The Inipi is a ceremony in itself, but it is also a very vital part of many of our other ceremonies. In our sun dance we go into the sweat lodge the first thing in the morning to cleanse ourselves before going into the circle. It helps us connect to that tree, that relative that stands in the center of the circle. At the end of the day, the last thing we do is go back into the sweat lodge. So the Inipi is the first and last thing we do every day of the sun dance. We also go into the Inipi before we go on the hill and when we come back down.

Originally, the Inipi was a men's ceremony. This was because of a

2. This is something I've been considering. There are many contemporary terms that I feel do not communicate the true idea. I might not use the terms *ritual* or *ceremony* too much longer.

man's lifestyle as the defender; he might have to kill to protect his family or his people, and that created a need for cleansing. A long time ago, when young men came home from a *zuya*, they would stop a mile or two from the main camp, and if one of them had taken a human life on that journey, his companions would paint his face black. They would bring him to the entrance of the main camp and stop, and his family would come out and take him into the Inipi to cleanse him. He had to do this before he'd be allowed back into the *tiośpaye*. The Inipi has many other uses, as I've mentioned, but that is one of them. Our Inipi is a wonderful ceremony.

The origin of the Inipi is told in a story about a woman who lived by herself. I don't know if I've ever told this story before. There were four brothers who lived together, and they were doing really well. Then one day a beautiful woman came and said, "I heard you brothers live by yourselves, so I've come to help. I've come to help you."[3] So the four brothers talked and decided to take her in as a sister. She began to live with them and help them. She made a home for them while they brought in the things that were needed to do that. She made a nice home for them, but then one day the oldest one left and didn't return. The second brother went looking for him, and he didn't return. This went on until the last brother was ready to go, and this woman begged him not to, but he said, "It's my responsibility to find my brothers." So he left, and then he didn't come back. One day as she sat on a hill, she remembered her brothers and began to cry. She looked down and noticed a little perfectly round pebble on the ground. She picked it up and put it in her mouth, just playing with it, rolling it around in her mouth, when she accidentally swallowed it. Swallowing that pebble made her pregnant, and soon she had a boy who grew very fast into a young man.[4] One day he wanted to know why she was alone, so she told him about his uncles.

After that, just as she feared, he asked her to make him some provisions and said that he was going to find his uncles. She begged

3. In a family, the woman is the keeper of the home. Everything in the home belongs to the woman, and the man provides so he will have a place to live.

4. This boy's name was Iŋyaŋ Hokśila, or Stone Boy.

him not to go, but he said, "That's why I came, to find them for you." So she made provisions for him and said, "That's the direction they went." He went in that direction for quite a while, and when he stopped to rest beneath a tree, a bird spoke to him. It said, "Yes, they came here, and they went in that direction." So he followed that direction until he came to another tree, and while he was resting there, another bird told him, "Yes, they came here. They went to that mountain." The bird said, "There will be a Wičaša waiting for you." (*Wičaša* is a term we use. It's a man. A Wičaša is a full-grown man, a mature man. We use that term to address different contacts; whether it's a spiritual contact or the sun dance tree, it's a Wičaša.) So the bird said, "There'll be a Wičaša waiting for you."

The young man got to the bottom of the mountain, and there was a bird. He said, "Yes, they came here, and they went to the top. When you get to the top, a little old lady will greet you. Be very careful. She will invite you into her lodge. In her lodge there will be four bundles, but be very careful, and when you finish what you have to do, build this lodge." The bird then gave him instructions on how to build the lodge. He said, "Heat ten stones. Take those bundles in the lodge and bring those heated stones in there and pour water."

So the man went to the top of the mountain, and this little old lady greeted him. She said, "Grandson, I've been waiting for you. I've prepared some stew for you. Come in and eat." So they went inside her lodge, and he looked around and saw the bundles lying there, and he was about to sit down when she said, "Grandson, now before you eat, could you walk on my back? I have a back problem, and when somebody walks on it, it feels better." She lay down on her stomach, and he went over to walk on her back, but when he looked at her, he saw that all along her spine were some sharp things protruding from her dress. This woman's name was Anogiṫe, Double Face Woman.

He stood next to her for a while and then turned himself into a

Sweat lodge • Oini.
A place to cleanse
and restore physical
and psychological life,
today commonly known
as a sweat lodge.

huge boulder and just rolled over her, crushing her to death. Then he turned back into a man and built the lodge. He covered it up as that Wičaša had instructed him and built a fire to heat the stones. Finally, he took those bundles in and then the hot stones. He poured the water on the stones, creating steam, and all of a sudden, those bundles began to move around. One of them said, "Let us out," so he untied the bundles, and they were his uncles. The old lady had tricked them into walking on her back to poison them and had bundled them up. So that's the story they told us about the Inipi.

I'd like to share a general description of the lodge and the ceremony. Roughly, you designate an area where you want to build your lodge, and you mark the center of that area, which will be the center of the earth. You make offerings on that space. I usually put a stick in the ground at that center, tie a rope a foot long or so, and make a perfect circle. Within that circle I take the earth out down to a foot or so. Then I take a few steps to the west and pile the dirt on that spot. I take a longer rope and go out four or five feet from the center and make a perfect circle, going around the hole I've just made.

On the west side where the doorway is going to be, I put two willows into the ground at an angle so they lean to the west at about forty-five degrees. I do the same on the east side and then bend those to the center, creating an arch with a bow in it. We bring them to waist level and tie them together and then do the same to the north and south sides and bend those over the other four that are already bent and tied. At that point, eight willows meet in the center, creating a dome-shaped structure. Sometimes between these sets of two there will be a space, and if I have enough willows, I'll put one or two willows in that space, bending them over and tying them in the center, just like the others. When I'm done, I'll have a dome-shaped structure. Then I'll take more willows, and from the inside, I'll go around the inside of the dome horizontally, about a third of the way up, going all the way around but leaving the doorway (to the west) open. I'll do the same a little farther up and then maybe a third row as well, so there aren't any large gaps or spaces. Then we cover the dome with blankets and then canvas tarps over the blankets to protect them from the weather. Then we make a door out of more blankets and canvas.

After that I step off some paces to the west of the altar (dirt from the center) and make a fire pit, maybe ten feet wide and a foot deep, piling the dirt around the pit. To make the fire, I'll put a platform in the middle of that pit, maybe four or five logs across with kindling underneath. I place the first seven rocks on the platform individually, first facing west, calling the relatives to be with this relative (stone) and help us, then to north, east, south, above, earth, then the seventh for myself, saying, "I am in this ceremony, and I ask this stone to be in this and work for us." Then I add as many rocks as we need. I often use twenty-four. I'll stack some dry wood around the platform, creating a pointed pyramid-shaped stack of wood, and then I offer tobacco to the Stone people, to the Tree nation, and to the fire and ask them to help the Stone relatives, to prepare them, so that when they come in, they will have what they need to help us. Once I make the tobacco offering, I start the fire.

A long time ago we used forked sticks, or antlers, to carry the stones into the lodge. Today we usually use a pitchfork. Once the stones are ready, we go into the lodge, moving clockwise. Each person says "Miṫaḳuye Oyas'iŋ" as they enter, addressing all creation that we are coming in there to be with them, to work with them, to address our needs in there. We are silent while the first seven stones are brought in, though we talk while the rest come in. Once the stones are in, the door is closed and the ceremony starts.

The Iniṗi can be a very intense ceremony; it's pitch-dark and done in close quarters. There are red-hot stones in front of us; all we can see with the door closed is the red glow of the stones. We ask people to relax, to welcome the heat and the stones, to talk to the stones in the center. Those relatives are there to help. Sometimes a medicine man will run the ceremony, and his spirit friends will be there to help us. The water and fire also help us.

There are four door openings, or four rounds, in the ceremony. We come out on the fourth. The length of time for the Iniṗi depends on how long people share in there. Some lodges are very long; others are short. It all depends on how many people talk in there and for how long. In each round, water is poured on the stones, creating hot steam. That water is there to help us. The lodge will last until the water is used up.

The Iniṗi opens your pores. You get rid of impurities in your body. We sing songs in there. Some are given by sprits and some are composed, and as we sing we cleanse our minds as well. The Iniṗi is a wonderful ceremony, and no matter how many times you participate, each one is different. Eventually, you will find yourself in there.

They always said that when we are dying, when we are physically or mentally weakened, we build our lodge, we heat the stones and the steam, and the Stone people will give life back to us, whether it's a physical need or a mental need. That's why when we go in that lodge, the people who conduct it will say, "Stay focused on the stones." The stones come from Iŋyaŋ, from the beginning when Iŋyaŋ completed creation and dried up and scattered all over the world. Those stones remind us of that. T̄uŋkaŋ Oyat̄e—that's the Stone people. *T̄uŋkaŋ* means "birth to now," "the beginning of time to now." And those stones remind us of that. We changed that term to *T̄uŋkaṡila*. So *T̄uŋkaŋ* becomes *t̄unka*, and *si* means "he or she is my adopted relative," and *la* is an expression of endearment. So that's how I would address each stone—T̄uŋkaṡila. Whether it's the spirit of the eagle, or the coyote, or the spider, whatever spirit comes in the lodge, I address them as T̄uŋkaṡila, also because they represent the beginning of time until today. And they are my relatives, and they are dear to me.

*chapter thirteen*

ORIGINS OF A GIFT

•

WOIHAŋBLE

In spite of all we have been through, our traditional philosophy continues. The main reason for this is that it went underground.[1] In the 1970s we had a psychologist working at the university, and he got a grant to study our *tiošpaye* system to determine if it still existed. Part of his study involved looking at our medicine men, and he helped organize them into the Medicine Men & Associates. As I remember, at that time there were about nineteen medicine men on the reservation who we didn't know existed. They had all gone underground, and their singers and family members had too. Most people had no idea they existed. As part of this organization of medicine men, each one had to record his vision, to tell how he received his gifts. I translated for many of these men and transcribed their explanations of these visions. They had never talked about their visions in public, but they said they would do so, so people wouldn't be afraid of them. They wanted people to understand our ceremonies and not fear them. Eventually, I asked if I could use their words in my classes, and they all said, "Sure. That's why we presented them in public."

I'm going to share some of their stories. I won't mention any names, but I want to give you an idea of how someone becomes a healer in our culture. I want you to have an idea of the responsibilities that come along with being a healer. There is a process that each of these men went through, and I'll share a few stories to give you the idea.

One medicine man told me that somebody came into his house at four thirty one morning. He said, "Somebody opened the door. The noise woke me up, and when I glanced at the clock, I saw that it was about four thirty. This person who had come in my house walked across the living room with real heavy steps, like a big man, and then the steps stopped at my bedroom door. I looked to see who it was, but there was no one there. Then a voice spoke up and said, 'I've come to give you a message.'" He said, "I looked closer, and here was this man about one foot tall, fully dressed, and about one foot tall. He came over to my bed and introduced himself and said, 'I've come to tell you that you have been selected.' He gave me a song and said, 'Sing this song. When you need my help, put ten rocks on the fire, heat them, sing this song, and call my name, and I will come, but to receive further instructions, you must fast on the hill for four days and four nights.[2] If you do, we'll give you instructions. You must do this soon, as soon as you can.' Then the man turned and left."

The medicine man told me, "I lay there for a long time—I don't know how long—wondering if I was dreaming, or if it really happened." He said, "I was doubting myself, thinking maybe I was imagining things, that I had dreamed it all up. I didn't do anything at first, but for several years this little man kept coming back, reminding me of what I needed to do. I was a young man, and I was scared, so I didn't do anything for eighteen years. I waited until I was fifty. By then they had begun to put a lot of pressure on me, so I finally went to a medicine man.[3] He said that he had seen me coming. He said, 'We've been waiting for you for quite a while.'" So the other

2. The ten rocks were for the Inipi. Our medicine men are the only ones who are mandated to haŋbleċeya for four days and four nights.

3. Usually the first contact these men have with the spirit is another man. When the spirits select someone, that man or woman will receive a visitor, a complete stranger. That visitor will tell them they have been selected and what they must do, but if they don't do it, the visitor will keep coming back, sometimes in the daytime, sometimes in dreams. They will say, "We are waiting for you. You must hurry."

medicine men already knew what he was supposed to do, but they couldn't say anything to him. He had to make his own decision to work with them.

The medicine man he went to see told him that he would sponsor him and take him through that process. First he took him into the Inipi to cleanse him. Only seven stones are used for these Inipis, and the door isn't opened until the water is used up. When the water is gone and the man is cleansed, the door is opened and all his supporters leave the lodge, but he stays inside and rubs himself with sage. At that point, no one is to speak to him, and he waits at the door. A quilt is put over his shoulders, and he either walks or is taken to the hill, still in silence. Often there will be some sort of protection for him where he is to *hanbleceya*, some simple sort of shelter. The altar is set up with flags of cotton cloth at each corner. The flags are about two yards long with a bundle of tobacco tied in one corner of the cloth. The southwest corner has a black flag, the northwest red. The northeast corner has a yellow flag, and the southeast is white. Chokecherry sticks at least seven feet long are stuck in the ground, and these flags are tied on them. To the west is another flag of red felt on a cedar branch stuck into the ground, stripped except at the top. A red felt with a tobacco bundle in the corner is tied to this branch. There is a green and a blue flag tied on chokecherry sticks stuck in the ground between the black flag and the red felt. Each medicine man asks for different numbers of tobacco ties, but however many are asked for, they must be on one continuous string and reach around the four corners of the altar. Often the same number of each color is made. The man going on the hill stands in the center, on the west side of his shelter, holding his *cannupa*. The medicine man will take that *cannupa* and ask his spirit friends to protect you, reminding you that you are on the most powerful part of the earth. He will sing a song for you, and if supporters are there, they will sing too, and when they leave, they are not to look back toward the man on the hill.[4] When you are standing on the hill, you become like those tobacco ties and flags. You are an offering. You are offering yourself. This is a general description, and each medicine man might have different little details, but this is basically how the *haŋbleċeya* is done. In the case of a medicine man, he will be up there for four days and four nights, and the man who initially contacted him will probably show up the first night.

The man who told me this story said that the first evening he was up, after everyone had gone, the coyotes were howling all around him, getting closer and closer, and then, all of a sudden, they were quiet. He said, "After a little while a man came to visit me, and here it was the same man that had been coming to my house for so many years." The visitor said, "Tomorrow morning at daybreak, when there is light to see, look to the north, over there. You will see a horse. Mark it well because under that horse's head is the dirt you need to fix your altar."[5] Then the visitor gave him further instructions—songs to sing and what kind of offerings he should make at his altar—and said, "Make these offerings and sing these songs, and I will come." Then the man turned and left.

Every day for four days, a different man came to visit the man on the hill. The next one to come said he represented the Elk and Deer nation. Again he gave instructions—what to put on the altar, how many flags and ties, what songs to sing. He said, "If you do this, I will come." Every day someone came. My friend said that all the while, right behind him, he could hear two people, a man and a woman, talking constantly. He said that every time he turned to get a look at them, they would move out of sight, and he was never able to see them.

This went on for four days and four nights. On his last day, in the afternoon before he was to come down, he said he was feeling really good, and a man came to him and said he was the eagle. He gave him instructions and said, "Now we're done." My friend said that this was about noon and that as soon as they were done, the pipe he

4. If they look back, they say you might be saying a final good-bye. For this reason, children are discouraged from coming up when someone is put on the hill.

5. To fix an altar is to set it up for a ceremony.

6. You stay on the hill until the medicine man and your supporters come to get you.

was holding became heavy, and he said, "All of a sudden, I was hungry and thirsty. I kept hoping they would come get me and take me down soon.[6] I was really suffering. It was really hot." He said right then he saw a little cloud off to the west, and he spoke to it and asked for help. He said, "I saw that cloud and said, 'I need some help,' and that cloud drifted over me and rained all around me, to the south, east, north, and west. It really cooled me off." He told me, "You know, all my life, ever since I was little, I heard stories about these things, but I never dreamed they would happen to me. When I experienced them, I wondered, 'Why me? I'm just a human being. That's all I am.'" He really questioned all that had happened to him.

They came to take him down that evening. They took him into the sweat to recount his experience, and that night they went into ceremony. He told the people what he experienced, and the spirit friend of the medicine man running the ceremony said, "What he said is true. We witnessed it." The medicine man told him, "Now you have your instructions. You know what you must do. You must do it soon to help the people." This man said he still waited. He was afraid and still wasn't quite sure about it, what to make of it all. Eventually, a man who had participated in the ceremony when he came off the hill offered him a pipe, so he accepted it and put on his first ceremony. He also invited the medicine man who had sponsored him on the hill to come and sit next to him during the ceremony.

He said, "I set that altar the way they showed me. I did everything they told me to do. I set the altar, sat down with all the offerings, and started to sing, and nothing happened. I kept singing and singing, and nothing happened. I thought maybe I was imagining it all, that maybe none of it was true." He said that as he was thinking these things, the medicine man sitting next to him leaned over and said, "Hey, keep concentrating. Put your faith into it." My friend said, "So I kept singing, and all of a sudden, this voice, this really high-pitched voice, spoke in my ear. This voice was speaking really, really fast, yet

I was able to hear every word clearly, and I could remember everything it said as well. And as soon as I began to hear this voice, things began to happen. Other spirits began to talk."

He said, "You know, that first year of doing ceremony, I was so excited. Every morning I would get up and step outside and think, 'I hope somebody will bring a pipe today.'"[7] He said the ceremonies were so energetic that he wanted to do them all the time. At the time he told us this story, he had been doing ceremony for nearly eighteen years, and he said he was tired. He said, "I'm really tired now. It's hard. I can't refuse a request, though sometimes I do, depending on what is being requested.[8] Most of the time I do the ceremony."

This man's spirit friends, when he went to do a ceremony, were the spider, the eagle, the coyote, the black-tailed deer, and the Heyoka, or contrary. Those were the spirits that came to him in ceremony. Some of them doctored, some helped in other ways, and they all had different offerings to be made for them.

Another man who recorded his vision said that he too had been selected to be a medicine man at a young age. He told us that many years later, he was working for a rancher on the western part of the reservation. He said he was way out on the ranch all alone, fixing fences. He said, "I was working in an opening on a hillside and looked up and saw this man coming towards me from down in the canyon. I could see it was a stranger, but for some reason, I wasn't afraid. That man came up to me and told me to come with him, that he wanted to show me something. I followed him to the ridge above us, and he told me to look across to the next ridge. I looked in that direction, and there was a Heyoka over there doing a ceremony. The man told me to look closely, to look really closely, and notice everything about the way the Heyoka performed that ceremony. I did that, and this man said to me again, 'Look closely at that Heyoka,' and when I did, I saw that it was me."

This medicine man said that when he was thirteen years old,

7. Bringing and offering a pipe to a medicine man is the protocol for requesting a ceremony.

8. Medicine men will refuse to do a ceremony if it is for a negative or harmful purpose.

he was playing in some old car bodies that were around his house. It was in the summer, and he said he got tired and lay down and went to sleep in the backseat of the car he was playing in. He said that while he was sleeping, a man came to him in a dream and gave him some instructions, and that when we woke up, he remembered everything clearly. He said, "I went back to my house all excited and told my parents about my dream, and they really chewed me out. They told me I was never to talk about that dream or those ways, that they were bad. They told me never to talk about it, so I didn't, but that man kept coming back for several nights while I was sleeping. It got so I was afraid to go to sleep."

He said that finally, that man stopped coming. For nearly five years he didn't come, and then, he said, "When I was eighteen, that same man came again. He told me the same things, gave me the same instructions. And by then I was running around with my friends and my girlfriend, partying and stuff like that, and I knew if I told my friends, they would just tease me and laugh at me. I didn't want that to happen, so I denied that dream again." He said the same thing happened: that man kept coming for a while and then stopped.

"That man stayed away for fifteen years, and then when I was thirty-three, he came back. By then I was really tired of it all and wondering why it was happening. It turned out that one of my uncles was very involved, secretly, in our ceremonies.[9] When I found that out, I told him what had been happening, and my uncle said I should have come to him sooner. My uncle said, 'Maybe it's not too late' and took me to another medicine man. This man looked at me and said, 'We've been waiting for you a long time.' He put me through some ceremonies, and it turned out that I was having a real vision, that I had to do that ceremony I had been shown."

This man said he used that Heyoka in ceremony a lot. He said, "When I was mending fences and shown that vision of the Heyoka doing the ceremony, I asked the man who had shown him to me why

9. Until 1978 ceremonies were done in secret because they were illegal.

he had come. He said, 'Every time you need my help, you call me, and I have never refused you, but you must do that ceremony in return for me.' He said that's why I had to do it."

So that's the way these men described their vision, how they received their gifts. They didn't seek them on the hill. They didn't seek to be medicine men, and they didn't seek their vision. It came to them. They used to talk about this. They would gather in an open forum on Rosebud and discuss these things. At one of these gatherings, one elderly medicine man told us that there are seven spirits that will select an individual, and once that individual has been selected, a visitor will appear to him or her. He said that's how it happens, that in Lakota philosophy people never seek powers or seek to be a medicine man. The spirits select whom they want. Other medicine men at this gathering described the same process. Also, they say that once you are selected, the spirits will never let you go. They say the only way they will let you go is if you pay their price, which is to give up whatever is closest to your heart. You must give up whatever you love the most in return for being let go.[10]

Another medicine man said that even though he knew it wasn't traditionally done, he really wanted to have a healing gift. He said that every summer he fasted on the hill for four days and four nights, asking for a gift. He said, "For ten years nothing happened, and then I went up again the next summer, for my eleventh year. I was up there again, and a man came and said, 'You don't give up. Every year we see you up here. We watch you, and every time you come up on the hill, you do everything the right way. You have a lot of faith, and because of that we will help you, but only with two things. There will only be two things you can do, so don't try to go beyond that.'" This medicine man said they gave him two gifts and that he was able to work with two illnesses after that. He told this story to a group of students as a teaching to them that they should never seek these gifts. He said that it was an enormous responsibility

10. One man told me he that when he was selected, he fasted for the hill for four days and nights and sun danced for four days for four summers, begging to be let go. They said no, unless he was willing to pay the price, so eventually he became a medicine man.

and that even with only two gifts, he was very tired. He said that if you're meant to be a medicine man, they will let you know. He's the only one I know of who went out to seek his gift and received it.

I think it's important to understand that these spirits we talk about, most are what are known in English as animals. We don't have a word for "animal" in Lakota, but that's what it is in English. The spirit friends come from those nations because they are relatives. They come to help us, to give us medicine.

• • •

Each medicine man has a different altar. Each altar is fixed differently. They each have different sets of tobacco ties and flags, and they each have different songs. Each one has his own songs. There are also songs that are more general and sung in all our ceremonies, but each medicine man has at least one specific song. A singer will study the altar when he goes to a ceremony. When the singers are invited to a ceremony, they will sit down and watch the medicine man fix his altar. An experienced singer can tell from the items that make up the altar just which songs to sing. They get their cues from the altar.

The process of becoming a medicine man always involves another medicine man. A recognized medicine man always looks to see if a person's vision is true, and this is because every one of us has the ability to create images in front of us. If you think of something hard enough, you can actually create that image in front of you. We can influence our dreams in the same way: we think about something so intensely that we begin to dream about it. Sometimes when we do this, the visions or dreams we create are so real that it worries and confuses us, and that's why we use this particular process. You go to a medicine man, and he will put you through a ceremony. He will work with his spirit friends to look at your vision, and even if that vision or dream was as clear as real life, he might tell you, "You are doing that to yourself. It's not a true vision." So that's the reason for the somewhat lengthy process used to confirm a true vision. If it turns out to be a true vision, then once that has been established, you start to do your ceremonies. It's a difficult process to go through, and it's a difficult life to lead.

I work with a lot of medicine men, and for the most part, they are pretty lonely men. People tend to avoid them because of their role. And they're like anyone else: they like to joke around and visit with others, but since people come to them for help, they see them in a different light and find it hard to relax around them. These medicine men tell me they feel like they are always on the spot, and they can't really associate with others the way they would like to. At one gathering, many of them said they wished people would just come and visit. One man said, "You know, we're just human like everybody else."

• • •

So that's how it is these days, but up until fifty or sixty years ago, our medicine men, our healers, were in a different category than they are today. Of course, they were people the same as the rest of us, and they were selected as I have described, but the healing process was different. In those days, healers would have a spirit friend that would possess them. That spirit friend would enter their bodies and take over during the ceremony. That spirit would do the doctoring through the healer.

One of my grandmothers was a healer, and she had the bluebird as her friend. This was in the 1940s, and she would do her ceremonies in a lighted room.[11] She said that when she sang her song, the bluebird would come in and heal the sickness she was treating. When she sang her song, and that bird came in, the people at the ceremony

11. Today our ceremonies are done in darkened, pitch-black rooms.

would hear a bird flying around the room and singing even though they couldn't see it. Eventually, that bluebird would enter my grandmother and would be singing out of her mouth, as if she were making the sounds. Then she would suck the sickness out of the patient's body, very similar to surgery. She would just suck the sickness out, and when she was done, the bluebird would be gone.

Another medicine man I knew would work with a round stone, with the Stone people. He would take a red-hot stone from a fire, glowing red, and roll it around and around in his hands. His spirits would be with him when he did this. After a while he would put the stone down and put his hands on the area of the body that held the illness and draw it out. He would take that illness out of the body with his hands.

So in those times the spirit would come in and possess the healer. That was the relationship that existed between them. The spirit would enter the healer's body and do the doctoring through them. When that last generation of healers died, however, around the 1940s or so, things went quiet for a while, and when the medicine men came back, they worked in a different way.[12] They practiced in the dark, and the spirits came in and did the doctoring without entering the healer.

Today our healers call themselves Iyeska, which means "interpreter" or "translator." In our ceremonies today, you talk to the spirit, and they answer you through the medicine man. They talk to him, and he translates. These men are able to talk to the spirits and to work with them only when they fix their altar. They sit in the center, the ceremony starts, and then they become Iyeska.[13] At that time, they have the ability to communicate with the spirits, but when the ceremony is over, the spirits leave, and the Iyeska puts his bundle away and becomes just like you and me.[14] He doesn't have any powers to heal. He's just an ordinary human being. The only time he's different is when he's sitting in that altar.

12. I want to say that what I am saying here is about the medicine men on the Rosebud Reservation. I'm not really sure about other areas and cannot speak about them.

13. When a medicine man fixes his altar, he sits before it, and that becomes the center of the ceremony.

14. A medicine man has songs to call the spirits, songs to say the offerings are made and asking them to receive the offerings. When they have received the offerings, the ceremony is over.

Someone asked me if healers were the same as medicine men. I think so, and today you hear both terms. Some of them say they are neither; they say we aren't healers, and we aren't medicine men. They say the spirits do the healing work and that they are Iyeska. In the days when the spirit would enter them, then you could say they were the healers because the healing came through them, but many don't feel that way today. And in those days they never went into public places. Their spirits were always around them, that energy was always around them, and if they went into a crowded space and walked by a woman in her monthly cycle, the energy would knock them out. So to avoid any commotion or embarrassment, they just stayed away from public places. Today it's different, and the Iyeska go anywhere they want because the spirit, that energy, is away from them unless they are in ceremony. The spirits come around only when they are called in ceremony.

One time I asked a group of medicine men if they thought the time would come when they would hold their ceremonies in a lighted room again. They all felt it might happen again, but only when the general public had a clear understanding and appreciation of our philosophy and our rituals. They felt that if they were to hold ceremonies in the light during these times, it would frighten people. One man said, "If we were to do that now, we'd probably scare everyone. They don't understand what we're doing anymore." We were in a classroom at the time and he said, "If we were sitting in here, and all of a sudden you heard a bird flying around the room or someone dancing on the table, but couldn't see anything, it would probably freak everybody out. If we all understood and appreciated that it's a spirit that has come in to help us, then it would probably feel good." I think this goes back to the concept of Mitakuye Oyas'iŋ, "all my relatives." If we understand that, then we see there isn't any mystery and that everything we do is reality based. We understand what we're doing, or at least we know what we're doing. Understanding comes after experience.

Sometimes a *tiošpaye* might have an herbalist, somebody who's gifted to work with plants. One herbalist I worked with said that she sometimes gets a feeling that she needs to go out on the prairie or down to the river and that as she walks along among the different plants, all of a sudden one of them will just stick out, very similar to someone in a crowd raising their hand and yelling, "Hey, over here!" She said that she would suddenly become attracted to one particular plant, and when that happened, she would go to it and make offerings. She would make offerings to all the plants of this earth and offer prayers that they would be healthy, and then she would take this plant that had called to her. These are the plants that become medicine. Herbalists are gifted that way. They have that special connection to that nation.

I mentioned that Iyeska are often lonely men. They have a very hard life. The first few years I sun danced, a couple of medicine men wanted to train me in the way of plants. I told them no, and when they asked me why, I said, "Because it's a big responsibility. I'm doing the best I can as it is, as I understand things, and I don't want to go beyond that." Part of my refusal had to do with how hard that life is. Sometimes, on the reservation today, we work with children of medicine men, especially their sons, and they often feel really neglected. A lot of them tell us that their dad pays more attention to other people than to his own children. It's kind of an occupational hazard, I guess, but these men get so busy as healers that they often don't pay enough attention to their own children. I don't think they do it intentionally, but it has the same effect on the kids, who get very upset.

So it's a very hard life, and pretty much all the medicine men I've worked with claim they didn't want that gift. One man I know, he's Heyoka, said that when he understood what was happening to him when he received his gifts, he went and sun danced for four years. He said that each of those years he fasted and danced for the four days of the dance, asking to be let go by the spirits. He said they finally said, "We'll let you go, but the price is whatever is closest to your heart." He said that when it came down to that, he gave in and began his life as a medicine man.

When you go into a ceremony, you have to remember that the spirits will respond to your request. They always say to be very careful of what you're thinking and what you're saying in ceremony. The spirits will listen to that, and they'll respond. That's why they say it's dangerous, and as I've mentioned before, as always the danger is us—not the spirits, not the medicine man, but us, the people. We are the danger because of what we might ask for.

I heard a story about a man who was a very gifted Iyeṡka. One of his brother-in-laws came to him and wanted to borrow some spirits from him. The medicine man said he couldn't go along with that, but his brother-in-law kept at him. Then his wife said, "He's your brother-in-law. Why don't you let him have them?" This man listened to his wife and finally gave in. He told his brother-in-law, "I'm going to tell two of them to travel with you, but you've got to do things right." His brother-in-law said of course he would, that he had respect for our ways. So the medicine man did what was asked and told two of his spirits to travel with his brother-in-law. Maybe two months later, in a ceremony, these two spirits came back and said, "We don't want to go around with that guy anymore. He's showing off, especially when there are a lot of women around. He'll set out some bottles and clap his hands, and we'll have to break those bottles. He's really showing off."

So the medicine man said, "Okay. Why don't you just stay here? Don't go back." He told his spirits to stay with him, but he didn't tell his brother-in-law that he had done that. Later on, there was a big gathering and a lot of people were there, and this man set up some bottles and stood before them and clapped his hands, but nothing happened. He walked around a bit and clapped again, but still nothing happened. He walked around some more, clapped again, and this time stomped his foot, but nothing happened. Finally, everyone who had come to watch him just walked away.

I think this story talks about something that's common in every culture. Wherever there is something good, there is abuse of that goodness. This goes back to the word *Wakaƞ*, and how every creation has good and bad in it. Sometimes the bad comes out, will show itself. In every creation there's a negative side as well as a good side.

Sometimes you see an individual carrying a medicine bundle. People often think a bundle gives them powers, but I asked a medicine man about this, and he said, "Sometimes the spirits will put some gifts in a medicine bundle through a ceremony, but the gifts are to help that person, the one who's carrying it. He cannot use that bundle to do ceremonies or influence others. Those gifts are just for his benefit." So carrying a medicine bundle does not give a person the right to do ceremonies.

This confusion around medicine and power is part of a bigger problem today. Many of us don't understand these ways anymore, and so we sometimes ridicule each other for practicing them, even down to what we wear. If I wear a choker on the reservation, people will make fun of me; if I wear it someplace else, people will respect it as part of our dress.

Even medicine men run into this problem. They say that when they travel to other places to do ceremony, the people really respect their altars, but when they're home, people just take them for granted. One man said, "We heat the stones, we load the pipe, and people are just joking around and not paying attention, but when we go to other places, people really respect what we're doing." I think this attitude among our people comes from our recent history and the resulting confusion about who we are. A friend was telling me he saw someone on the reservation wearing an eagle feather and didn't think that man should have been dressing like that. I said to him, "Why not? How come you don't have the same feelings when you see someone wearing a cross? That feather is a symbol of our beliefs." So I think it's this general attitude that prevents us from understanding and practicing our beliefs, but now that we're doing more of these things, we try to explain what we're doing to the young people so they will have respect.

If you go to the ceremony of a true medicine man, he will explain how he came to be a healer. He will talk about his vision. He will tell you who his spirit friends are. The true ones all go through that process I described to make sure their dreams or visions were true. And again, that's because of the ability we all have to create images in front of us or influence our dreams. Our healers are really challenged as they go through that process. One man told me that he was on the hill for four days and nights, and on the third day he was really hungry. Just starving. He said, "I looked up, and here somebody was coming toward me. It was a woman, and she said she had heard me up there and wanted to help. She said, 'Cousin, I want to help you along, so you will finish your *haŋbleċeya*. I brought this for you,' and she held out a bowl of soup." He said, "I was just so thankful that one of my relatives had brought me something to eat, but when I reached for it, I remembered I wasn't supposed to eat. I held back and told her no, and that woman just disappeared right in front of me."

So men who have been chosen to be healers are really challenged. One told me he heard a voice say, "If you don't get off this hill, you'll die." You have to have faith to stay with it. You really have to believe in that pipe. Another man told me that when he was on the hill, the first night, all night long, a woman behind him was laughing. He said it was a woman's voice, but it wasn't a human sound. The second night, just before sunset, he came down off the hill. He said, "I just couldn't take another night of that. It was too much." So he gave up and came down.[15]

15. While medicine men are really challenged, these stories tell about the type of challenge anyone might face on the hill. They're not specific to medicine men.

There are other pressures that arise when you're fasting. Sounds get sharper. After two days of fasting, your senses get sharp. You hear things you've never heard before. We shut out so many of the sounds that are usually around us, but after fasting for a few days, you hear them all. It can be overwhelming. And your sense of smell sharpens, too. You can smell something cooking a mile away, and after two or three days of no food and water, that can be really hard.

I want to say that rituals like the *haŋbleċeya* are not just for medicine men. They are for all of us, and they are designed to help you find yourself, to find out where you stand. They say that if you decide to do them, you must do them for four years. If you decide to *haŋbleċeya*, you must do it for four years, so it's important to prepare properly. Some people will prepare for one or two years to understand what they are going to do. It's a difficult ceremony; it's hard being up there without food and water. When it's raining or cold and blowing hard, you have to contend with that, and it's difficult to meditate or reflect. Once I was up there, and I had a nice spot, but whenever I dozed off, one of the flags would pop, just like somebody was snapping a towel. Right behind me, that flag would snap and wake me up. It got really cold that night, and I'd wrap up in my quilt, but every time I dozed off, that flag would snap and wake me up, so I finally said, "Okay!" So things like that happen to tell you that they're present. They're listening to your prayers.

And, you know, how you are challenged doesn't depend on the length of time you're up there on the hill. A friend of mine was going up for one night, and he hadn't bothered to prepare his spot. The morning he was going up was just beautiful, and he wasn't feeling like it was going to be much of a challenge. I told him there was still plenty of time to prepare, but he said, "No, it's just for one night, you know."[16] That afternoon the clouds started to come in, and by the time we took him up, it had started to rain. It rained all night, the

16. Some of our medicine men allow us to prepare the spot where we will *haŋbleċeya*. We might put up a small shelter of branches for shade.

wind blew, and it was cold. The next day, in the evening, we went to get him, and he looked beat. He said he almost walked out of there during the night. He said, "I learned my lesson. You shouldn't say, 'It's *just* one night.' They'll really challenge you."

The elders understood how to talk to the spirits better than we do, and they always said to never ask the spirits what you should do. If you need to ask them for help, find a way to say what you will do in return for their help, but never ask them what you should do. If you state what you'll do in return, they'll appreciate it, and if you simply ask, they might give you something to do that seems simple but will be very hard for you. One medicine man told me a story about a friend of his who sold some land and made a lot of money. He decided to put on a ceremony to give thanks, and when the ceremony started, this spirit came in and was going around to people saying, "Hau, Hau." The man who sponsored the ceremony said, "Hau, Ḱola" (Hello, friend), and that spirit immediately went over to him.[17] That man got very excited, and he said, "Ḱola, I come prepared. Whatever you want, I'm ready." This man's wife nudged him and told him not to speak like that, but he said, "Woman, keep quiet. I'm talking to my Ḱola." And he said it again ... "Whatever you want, I'm ready." This went on, and the man's wife was trying to reason with him, but he'd made a lot of money and was pretty full of himself. He felt he could do whatever the spirit asked. So the spirit was quiet for a bit, and then the medicine man said, "Ḱola wants to know if you know that hill that's west of Bead's Dam. There are fourteen graves on that hill." This man said, "Oh, yes. I grew up around here and know where it is. I know that place." "Well," said the medicine man, "your Ḱola wants you to do the haŋbleċeya there for eight summers." This man went quiet for a long time, and then said, 'Ṫuŋḱaṡila, are you talking to me?" So that's pretty funny, but it makes a point: you never ask them what you should do. This man had to do exactly what he ask for.

17. *Hau* (hello) is a male form of greeting, an oral expression made by men for greeting or affirming. *Ḱola* is "friend," again the male form of expression. Generally, a woman would never initiate a greeting to a man. If she did, however, she would do so with a relative term, such as *Tiblo* (older brother) or *Misuŋ* (younger brother). To such a greeting, a man would reply, "Hau, Ṫaŋḱṡi" (younger sister) or whatever relative term is appropriate.

• • •

Each healer has a different altar, as I mentioned. Each healer has his own set of spirits. One healer will have this set of spirits; another will work with a different set. The plants that healers use will be selected by their spirits. The medicine they give to people is selected by their spirits. And a true medicine man will not allow anybody to put a curse on anyone else. They will tell you they are there to help. If you take a pipe to a medicine man and say you want to do a ceremony to affect another person negatively, they won't take the pipe. They won't smoke that pipe and do that ceremony.

The majority of medicine men won't do a ceremony to look for a lost person or object, either, because the price of this is so high. The price to the medicine man isn't high, but the price you pay to the spirits is too high. I heard of one family that lost a daughter. She was gone for several weeks, and finally her parents went to a medicine man, and in the ceremony the spirits told them they had to make a decision. They said they could find the missing daughter. They also said that when they found her, if she was not alive, they didn't want anything, but if they found her and she was still alive, the price was whatever was closest to her parents' heart. They told the parents to go home for the night and think about that decision before making their choice. The next night, the family came back and said they didn't want to go through with it. They didn't want the spirits to look for their daughter. Two weeks later, the daughter called home. She was in Chicago with some friends. Most medicine men won't do this kind of ceremony; the price to the spirits is so high.

Again, remember that you are working with relatives. It's the same as if you express your needs to a roomful of your friends. In that case, someone might say they can help, that they have what you need and can help. Someone else might know of some other person who can help you. It's the same thing in ceremony, but in there you are talking to spirits, and they can do things we can't. They can work wonders, so you have to be careful what you ask for. They know the plants. They know the medicines. They have resources we don't have, and they really know how to get things done.

If you're invited to a ceremony where you haven't been before, you should ask someone who has how to behave in there. You should find out as much as you can beforehand, so you won't be confused or frightened in there. It can be scary if you haven't experienced it. You go in that ceremony room, and it's pitch-black, the singing is very loud, and there are sounds and lights. It can be scary, and it's always interesting.

One of our medicine men went to Europe, to Austria, and it was a crowded ceremony. A lot of people came, and toward the end, the medicine man told the group, "When they sing the next song, those of you who need help, they'll help you in appreciation for being invited here." So the singers began the song, and about halfway through it, a woman in the group started screaming and screaming. The medicine man stopped the singing and told the spirits to leave. Then he said to turn on the lights in the room. When the lights came on, there was a woman who was terrified, sitting there wild-eyed and wanting to know where she was. They told her where she was, and eventually she calmed down a little. They explained that she was at a ceremony, and she looked around and asked what day it was. When they told her, she was quiet for a bit, and then said, "According to what you say, I have been asleep for eighteen years." She said, "I went to sleep almost eighteen years ago and just woke up." It turned out that a spirit had taken her over eighteen years before that night, and when the medicine man's spirits came in to doctor the people, they took that spirit out of her. She said that all of sudden she woke up, and she was in a pitch-dark space with all this drumming and strange singing and other noises. She didn't know where she was, so she started screaming. She'd been gone for nearly eighteen years. That's an unusual story, but these things do happen.

.  .  .

I'm sharing these stories so you might have a good understanding of our philosophy, our medicine men, and our rituals. So you won't be afraid of them. That was the hope of the medicine men who told these stories in the first place. They wanted people to understand and not be afraid. I'm not on a mission; I'm not trying to convert people, but I do want people to understand who we are and what we do. I want people to understand. There are so many misconceptions about us. A few years ago a young girl about twelve years old asked me when I would start growing feathers. Another fellow asked me if it rains every time I dance. There are just so many misconceptions out there.

*chapter fourteen*

# THE CONTRARY

•

# HEYOKA

I've shared my experience with our medicine men to the best of my knowledge and understanding. I've shared from what they have told me, what I have witnessed, and what I have experienced. Now I'd like to share a little bit about one particular role that is a little unusual, but I think it probably exists in every culture in one form or another. That is the role of the Heyoka oyate, the contrary. There might be a word for this role in English, it may even be *contrary*, but these spirits embody the opposite of what is thought of as standard or normal. They embody the opposite of that cultural standard. In Lakota culture, that spirit comes from the Wakiyaŋ oyate, the Thunder nation. It's the opposite of everything that we believe is normal. When that spirit says yes, it means no. When it says no, it means yes. Whatever they say, they mean the opposite. We call that spirit a Heyoka.

I'm not going to say too much, because to this day Heyoka is a very touchy subject. The church has attached so much mystery and sacredness to it that people are afraid. Even though they don't really understand what it is, they are afraid of the Heyoka. From what I have learned, however, it's a very clear situation concerning a man or woman who is contacted by the thunder spirit, the Heyoka. That spirit will approach them and will help them in their ceremonies.

A long time ago our people would respond to that because they'd know, they'd know and understand exactly what it was. They would know that the contrary is also a natural part of our life, of our way of life. But when Christianity came in, from the beginning of that presence here, all of our spirits were considered evil, so people who experienced those things, particularly the Heyoka, were also considered bad or evil. Our people became afraid. I've mentioned that Christianity used the word *sacred*, and if something was sacred, then it became something you couldn't touch but would have to bow to and worship. That's what they taught us about anything that was sacred. So they introduced that word, that concept, to us, but as I've said throughout this book, in our culture everything is a relative regardless of the situation. Everything is a relative, and we work with them all.

They always said that a Heyoka spirit will come into the altar of a medicine man. He'll do ceremonies with that Heyoka, but working with that spirit doesn't make that man Heyoka; it just makes the association with that Heyoka spirit. Having a Heyoka as a spirit friend can make for a difficult life, and it's difficult to make that relationship work if you are visited. One medicine man told me his mother was visited, but she didn't want to make that association. He said that whenever a storm came up, she would cover all the windows and sit in the house with a child on her lap because the Heyoka would never touch a child. So she'd sit there all through the storm with a child on her lap, but one time she was sitting there like that, and there was a little nail hole in the wall, and lightning came through that hole and just grazed her arm. They wanted to show her they could get at her. It's a very demanding calling.

There are also Heyokas that aren't medicine men but use laughter as a medicine. Rodeo clowns are Heyokas, carnival clowns, making people laugh. That's one role of a Heyoka. There are also Heyokas who don't do ceremonies or healing of any kind. They live alone and don't associate with people. I don't know too much about them, and I've never seen one, but one of my uncles knew one, and he told me this story. One day my uncle told his wife, "I want you to make some real hot stew and fix up a bed. I'm going to invite the Heyoka for the night. I feel bad about the way he lives and want to do something for him." So my aunt prepared the meal and made up a bed. This was in February. There was a ground blizzard going on, and it was really cold. My uncle got on his horse and went to the Heyoka's place and found that the man had just a little lean-to, a little shelter, and a tiny fire. He found him heating up something to eat and just barely dressed. He said, "I want you to come to my house tonight and have a nice hot meal and stay there." The Heyoka said, "I can't do that," and my uncle asked him again, saying, "If you come with me, it will make me feel better." So the Heyoka said he would go with him if it would make him feel better, and they went back to my uncle's house together. It was a one-room log building and all warmed up inside. The table was ready and they sat down to eat, and that Heyoka got colder and colder the warmer it got inside. Finally, he was just sitting there shivering. My aunt kept feeding the stove, thinking he was cold because he was barely dressed, but he just got colder and colder. After the meal, my uncle said, "Now I want you to stay here tonight. We've fixed a nice bed for you." The Heyoka said he'd stay, but only if they put a coat on the floor by the door. He said he'd rather sleep there. So my uncle said, "No, I want you to sleep in a bed. It's going to make us feel better." The Heyoka said in that case, he'd sleep in the bed, and he did, but he had nightmares all night. He couldn't sleep at all. So that's how it is for a Heyoka. My uncle said that in the summertime, this man would be bundled up, trying to stay warm, and then in the cold of winter he'd be barely dressed and hot all the time. But that behavior is real: it's their nature; they're not acting.

The word *Heyoka* can refer to a man or a woman, or to the spirit. It depends on the situation. If there is a gathering and a Heyoka is there, it would be the person. I have a photo of an elderly woman, and one of my older cousins looked at that picture and said, "Oh, that's the Heyoka Wiŋyaŋ" (the Heyoka woman). I had heard that at one time there had been an elderly woman who was a Heyoka, and then I heard a story about her when she was at a gathering that took place around here every spring or summer. The people would come and sit in a circle, and different healers would come out and demonstrate their gifts. That way people would know who they were and what gifts they had. So one time at this gathering, this particular woman came out and put a tumbleweed in the center of the circle. She stuck it in the center of the circle and began to walk around singing, and little flowers popped up on the branches of the tumbleweed. She took these flowers and gave them to people who needed medicine.

As I mentioned, today many people are afraid of Heyokas, and I think that fear comes from Christianity. Heyokas are a natural part of life, and until we were taught they were evil, we weren't afraid of them. Also today, there are some people who, if they aren't afraid, have a lot of romantic thinking about Heyokas and seek to become one. Mostly, I think that comes from wanting recognition. They are people seeking attention. You get to wear masks and do crazy things. When anyone puts on a mask, they become entirely different in their behavior. Medicine men who work with the Heyoka, however, feel very thankful that they don't have to live that Heyoka lifestyle. They respect and honor it and are very thankful they don't have to live it. They always say that if you are going to talk to that Heyoka spirit, have the eagle or the coyote interpret your prayers so that you don't make a mistake in talking to them. Those nations will speak your prayers to the Heyoka in a clear way if you ask them to.

So the Heyoka is real life. It may be the complete opposite of what we think of as normal, but it's real life and it's natural. It's not pretend, and it's not something to be feared. It should be respected. If anyone is claiming to be Heyoka, I hope they really try to understand what it is. If they do, they might approach it differently. They might correct their behavior. They could easily be misleading themselves.

*chapter fifteen*

# MY FIRST CEREMONY

•

## ṪOḰALAḢĊI LOḰOL WOEĊUŋ EL WAI

The first ceremony I participated in was the Iniṗi, and before I end this book, I want to tell my story of coming (back) to that moment. Bits and pieces of this story have been mentioned throughout this book, but I want to bring it into focus here; it may be helpful for others who are in a similar position today. It's important to say that at this point in our history, we are all coming back. I'm thankful that there is still anything to come back to. So we all have to examine ourselves honestly, look back over our lives and our influences, and then start from where we are. That process began for me in my early years.

I received no real education until I was sixteen years old, and today I feel fortunate because of that. I went to a government day school where we weren't taught anything. We were just there. In 1949 one of my brothers and two other men took a petition to the Tribal Council to adopt the South Dakota State Code of Education, and in 1950 when the tribe adopted that petition, the State Board of Regents came in and found that only one man out of all the teachers on the reservation had the credentials to be certified as a teacher. So while there were government day schools, they weren't effective and didn't really teach us anything. There were a number of them, one in Spring Creek, one in Soldier Creek, in Horse Creek, and some are still there. They still exist in He Dog and Oak Creek (today called Okreek). Back then, however, teachers hired by the government taught at all of those schools, and none of them were certified. So I didn't even learn English in that school, but all during this time I was growing up in a small community where only Lakota was spoken. I never heard anything but Lakota, and in the evenings there was storytelling. That was my education.

When I was sixteen, I graduated from that day school, from the eighth grade, and was told I couldn't go back to school after that. In those days, according to state law, when you were sixteen, you didn't have to go to school anymore. So I was living at home back in our little community and after a while began to think that I'd like to go to school in St. Francis, to the boarding school there. My mother never wanted me to go to school at all; she was happy that I was back home and really against me going to St. Francis. Eventually, though, she gave in and took me there, and that was when I found out that I barely spoke English, that I had no Western education at all. I stayed at St. Francis until I graduated from boarding school at age twenty.

An important piece of this story is that my father was a catechist.[1] He was orphaned when he was an infant, and his mother, my grandmother, married a man named White Hat, who unofficially adopted my father. White Hat was strong in the church, so my father practically grew up there as well. He worked for the mission and was a very dedicated man. He had strong faith. He died when I was about four years old, but I still remember him fixing his harnesses for the horses. I also remember him from when my mom lifted me up when he was in his casket. They told me that after they buried him, after they covered up the casket with earth, that I sat on the grave and wouldn't

1. Generally, a lay minister trained in the art of religious instruction.

move. They said they had a hard time pulling me off his grave, but I don't remember that. Those are my only memories of my father.

My oldest brother volunteered for the army during World War II. My father died while my brother was in service. My next older brother was sixteen. Mom had to rely on someone for survival, and as my father was a catechist, she had gone to church with him. Sometimes the priest would give her groceries and help her, so she continued to go to church after his death. I believe she was faithful to both traditions, the church and our traditional practices.

She said my father was so giving that he never accumulated anything. There was one story about when the cattle were brought in the first time.[2] So Mom's brothers and cousins—Iron Shell and Hollow Horn Bear—brought a nice fat steer to Mom and said, "We got this for you 'cause we know that Joe [my dad] is going to get the worst one for himself. He's going to give the best and bring home the worst." And sure enough, that's what he did. I guess that's the kind of guy he was.

There are other stories about him. One man told me that my father healed him from being a hunchback. He said, "When I was nine years old, I had an accident, and I was hunched over really bad. I couldn't straighten up. I couldn't do anything. Your father would come by on horseback every Sunday. He'd take me to that country church, and we'd kneel at that altar, and he'd pray from that black book." (In those days the Catholics had a black book where all the prayers were translated into Lakota.) "He'd pray from that book and sing hymns. Every Sunday. One Sunday we were in there, and he prayed and was singing a song, and my back began to straighten up until it was completely healed." He said, "I've laid cement blocks all my life and never had any back trouble again. The church told him to never talk about that healing, but your father had that kind of faith."[3]

Throughout her life, my mom always told stories about her family, about Hollow Horn Bear. She told about Hollow Horn Bear and

2. Herds of cattle were brought in by the government and distributed to the people, one to a family. Many of us had to get used to beef; it made us sick at first.

3. From stories like that, I've come to believe that whatever faith you have, if you put your heart into it, somebody is going to respond. Something is going to respond and help you.

his brothers, what they accomplished, what skirmishes they were in, stories like that. I really enjoyed those stories and also liked the stories of the *zuya*, when she described where those young men went and what they did. Those stories never left my mind. Also, I remember the times when I was a boy in the 1940s and my uncles and aunts would come to our place and have a sweat ceremony. They'd always take the lodge apart afterward, to avoid getting caught, and then they'd have a little potluck meal. By the time I graduated from St. Francis in 1959, however, I didn't see any more of that life. It seemed to be gone, and by the 1960s, I was wondering if we'd ever do any of that again.

I mentioned my trip to Dallas after high school; after that I came back home and worked on ranches and rodeoed. I went to California in the late '60s to look for work, but decided I needed to make something of myself in my own home and came back to Rosebud in 1969. It was about that time that I found the medicine men who were still left.

The first ceremony I participated in was just by accident, and I was in my early thirties. There was a man I had worked with on various tribal programs, and I had heard he was a medicine man. One time I had a visitor who wanted to meet a medicine man, so I took her to meet him. When we got to his place he said, "You're just in time." I said, "For what?" and he said, "We're going to have a sweat." Though I'd seen sweats done when I was a boy, I'd never done it, but he gave me a towel, and I joined in.

I didn't know anything. By that time in my life, I was basically coming from a Christian orientation, and the only prayer I knew was the Our Father, so that's what I started praying. When they brought the rocks in, it got really hot, and I was really praying those Our Fathers. And I didn't know about the hot steam that comes off the rocks and burned my throat because I sat up tall and breathed in when they poured the water. Even with all that, I stayed in that lodge, and something about it really grabbed me, really pulled me in.

The next day, I went back for another Inipi and watched more closely. I saw that the other men bent down as the steam came off the rocks, so I did the same, and the steam went over my head. It all felt really good, and I came out of that lodge feeling great, but when I sat down, I passed out. It knocked me out cold.

Then I started going back as often as I could, trying to learn and understand, and it took everything I had in me to do that. I'd had so much Christian teaching and been taught that those traditional practices were evil. By then most of our people condemned our traditions altogether. All of my relatives were devout Christians, and they condemned them too. I didn't tell anybody what I was doing, and it took me a while to really immerse myself in it and convince myself that it was all right, that it was good. I was only able to do that because of what I learned from my mother. That's what kept me going, and then the medicine men began to welcome me more and more. I found out that many of them were my relatives and that they were eager to share and looked for people to share with, but, unfortunately, at that time there was little response. These men and their families were happy to see me, and they started teaching me songs. I didn't know any of our songs. I want to say that nothing about this process was easy: even though I liked the experience, it was really hard. I had to overcome a lot of negative conditioning to convince myself that it was all right. I'm glad I stayed with it.

So much had changed since I was a boy. I saw some ceremonies when I was young, but like any young person, I didn't really pay any attention. Even in the 1960s, I didn't know our practices were against the law. I did notice the medicine men were very cautious around the ceremonies, and in welcoming me in, and then when I started working as a teacher, I did some research and found out it was all against the law. About that time, some of our men challenged that law. There was a Cheyenne man; there were Lame Deer and Fools Crow and some others. They came forward with these practices, and our people were terrified but also drawn to them. I was thankful those guys came out and demonstrated what it all was.

A lot of those men were the ones who later formed the Medicine Men & Associates. They were our medicine men here on Rosebud. After a while, one of them said to me, "Spend a month with me, and I'll teach you everything you need to know about the medicine." By that time I had been working with some of the medicine men, singing for them and helping them lead the sun dance, and he said, "I heard what you are doing" (he called me Misuŋ, a relative term), "and I'll teach you everything about the plants, the roots, everything you need to know. Spend a month with me." I thought about that offer and went back to him and told him no. He asked me why, and I said, "I don't want that responsibility. I know myself, and I don't want that responsibility." He said, "Well, I'm glad you're honest about it." So I never tried that. Even from the beginning, for some reason, I didn't want to become a medicine man. I could have done some of those things, but it's just not for me.

So I want to close by saying how much I appreciate the gift that was given to me by these men and women. I was orphaned at the age of sixteen. My father died when I was four, and Mom died when I was sixteen, but they established a foundation for me with my relatives. They took the time to correct me and talk to me, and they always introduced me to relatives using a relative term.

When the medicine men took me in to work with them, it was the greatest gift I could have ever received. It changed my life. When I graduated from high school, I thought these men and our ways were gone for sure. I didn't know there were any medicine men still left. By then everybody denied who they were, denied they were even Indian, much less medicine men. Our people were ashamed. There was nearly 100 percent alcoholism on the reservation. Families were all spread out and separated. My family was all over the place, and I wondered if anything my mom had taught me still existed. But then

I found it, just a trace of it, and her stories came back to me very strong.

When I first stepped into it, the medicine men were very cautious around me, and it was a while before I realized this was because our practices were against the law. After about three years, however, they really took me in and taught me many things. They encouraged me to share that knowledge with people who don't speak Lakota. They wanted me to share with those who came seeking an understanding. They didn't want that confusion, misunderstanding, and abuse of our way of life to continue, and they felt the way to protect our practices was through knowledge and understanding.

That's why they formed the Medicine Men & Associates and taught their course, which is a great deal of what I have presented in this book. They said, "If people know us and know who we are, they won't be afraid. They will understand who we are. They will discover the beauty of who we are and what we do." To create this understanding, they spoke openly of their dreams, their communications with the spirits, of the ceremonies, and they had never done this before. I transcribed their talks and gave some of them a transcription, so they could have a written copy of their personal stories. One medicine man, when we had visitors from outside who came for ceremony, would come to that ceremony and ask somebody, one of us, to read that transcription of his story. He wanted people to know what the ceremony was about, who the spirits were.

So some of the medicine men had copies of their own stories, their own dreams and visions, in writing. I did this happily, learning from them, and they encouraged me to share their stories and their teaching with others. Then they asked me to run a sun dance. They said, "This is your home. This is where you belong." I thought it over, and when I told them I would and how I wanted to run it, they supported me. They came to my dance each year, supporting what we were doing.

I'm not a medicine man. I don't consider myself a spiritual leader. I practice what I believe the best I can. I learned these beliefs first from my mother and then from our medicine men. I'm sharing this in written form because I don't have much time to go on, and I hope, in reading this, that people will have a better understanding of who we are. Our own people, even my own children, will be able to understand the importance of our culture, our way of life, and how we can use that to save not only ourselves but maybe our grandmother, the earth, and all that is around us. That's why I have written this book, and I hope it will help.

So, with that, I just want to say thank you pilamayapelo.

*Appendix A*

## FAMILY MEMBER AND RELATIVE TERMS
·
## WOŦAK̄UYE

I'd like to make a very brief presentation of some of our family member and relative terms, many of which have been used in this book. In our culture we address each other as relatives, and we use these terms. We do this to show respect and to practice the Miŧak̄uye Oyas'iŋ concept. This is only a partial list of our relative terms, but I wanted to give you an example of how they are used. If you would like more information on these terms, please take a look at my earlier book, *Reading and Writing the Lakota Language: Lakota Iyap̄i Uŋ Wowap̄i Nahaŋ Yawap̄i.*

Our word for father is *Aŧe*, and for mother it's *Ina*. Their son is *Ćiŋkśi*, and their daughter is *Ćuŋkśi*. Aŧe and Ina call their children Ćiŋkśi and Ćuŋkśi, and they, in turn, call their parents Aŧe and Ina. Those are the terms for our nuclear family.

If Aŧe has older brothers, he will call them Ćiye and his younger brothers Misuŋ (or Misuŋk̄ala). Ćiŋkśi and Ćuŋkśi will address these men, who in English would be uncles, as Aŧe, which means "father," and they will be like fathers to them. If Aŧe has sisters, he will call his older sisters Ṫaŋke and his younger sisters Ṫaŋkśi. Ċiŋkśi and Ċuŋkśi will address these women as Ṫuŋwiŋ. This word means "birth woman" or "a woman who gives birth." In English these women would be aunts.

If Ina has sisters, she will call the older sisters Ċuwe and the younger Miṫaŋ (or Miṫaŋkala). Ċiŋkśi and Ċuŋkśi will address these women, who in English would be aunts, as Ina, which means "mother," and they will be like mothers to them. If Ina has brothers, she will call her older brothers Tiblo and her younger brothers Misuŋ (or Misuŋkala). Ċiŋkśi and Ċuŋkśi will address these men as Lekśi. In English these men would be uncles.

Lekśi and Ṫuŋwiŋ will call their nephews Ṫuŋśka and their nieces Ṫuŋjaŋ. These are simply other terms for son and daughter. If one of Aṫe's sisters is married, then Aṫe's children will call that sister Ina and her husband Aṫeṫela, which is another term for father. Grandfathers are most commonly called Ḳaḳala or Lala. Sometimes they are called Ṫuŋkaśila, but this is a more formal, very respectful term applied to a grandfather who has gained wisdom and lives by it. He is a man of respect. A grandfather's brothers, male cousins, and brothers-in-law are all Ḳaḳala or Lala to Ċiŋkśi or Ċuŋkśi. They are exactly like a natural grandfather.

Grandmothers are called Ḳuŋśi or Uŋċi. Her sisters, female cousins, and sisters-in-law are all Ḳuŋśi or Uŋċi to Ċiŋkśi or Ċuŋkśi. They are exactly like a natural grandmother.

In our culture, children of either sex call an uncle Lekśi and an aunt Ṫuŋwiŋ. *Uncle* and *aunt* are the closest translations into English, but in Lakota "Lekśi" and "Ṫuŋwiŋ" are really just another way of saying "father" and "mother." It seems to me that in Western thinking, there is some emotional and psychological distance between the way a child sees its parents and the way it sees its uncles and aunts. In Lakota this is not the case. Saying "Lekśi" is like saying "Aṫe." Saying "Ṫuŋwiŋ" is like saying "Ina." Different terms are used only to distinguish them from biological fathers and mothers, but these terms do not imply any difference in the relationship with the child.

Also, we have no concept of orphan in Lakota culture. Our word *Wableniča* means "one who no longer has any biological parents," but it's only a description of a situation. There are other sets of parents for that child, aunts and uncles, and no psychological distance, as in English. They are the same as your biological parents. Everyone in a *tiošpaye* practiced the same lifestyle, and if your biological parents died, you would be raised by your uncles and aunts in exactly the same way as you had been in your biological family.

$\psi$

*Appendix B*

## WORKING WITH OUR HEALERS

·

## UŊK̇IṪA WAK̇AŊ IYESK̇A OB WOWAŚI EĊUŊK'UŊP̄I

There are certain things we must do to work with our healers. If you want to sponsor a ceremony for yourself or for somebody else, first you would smudge the space, yourself, and your pipe.[1] Then you would load your pipe with prayers for the type of ceremony you want to sponsor; you would put those prayers into your pipe. You need to put seven pinches of tobacco into your pipe. They are for the six directions and then a seventh pinch that represents you. That pinch is the one that represents that you will take responsibility for your problem and for the help you seek. So you load your pipe with those prayers and roll up a little ball of sage to cap it. When the pipe is loaded, you cap it with a ball of sage to keep other influences from going into that pipe. Then you take your loaded pipe to the medicine man you want to work with. You tell him why you have come, that you have come to ask for a ceremony, and explain the problem and the (type of) ceremony you want. When you have done this, offer him the pipe, and if he takes it from you and smokes it, it means he will do the ceremony.[2] After the pipe is smoked, he

1. If you don't have a pipe, you might ask the medicine man for one to use.

2. Medicine men are not obligated to take the pipe, though they will usually do so unless they feel they are not the ones to do your ceremony, or if you are asking for something with a negative or harmful purpose.

will set the time and place for the ceremony, and then you need to ask whatever questions you might have. It is important to ask how many people might come, besides those you are inviting, as it is your responsibility to feed them. If he says maybe fifteen people, then you should probably prepare food for twice that number, because there are always more people than you expect. You prepare a basic meal, maybe a beef stew or something like that; whatever the people normally eat, that's what you prepare for the ceremony. You might ask the medicine man or his wife what people usually bring and then prepare that.

There might be several sets of tobacco ties needed, so you should ask about that—how many sets, what colors, and how many of each color. Ask about the flags he needs and whether you need felt as well.[3] If you don't know about these things, you can simply ask him what you need to bring for the altar, and he will tell you. On the night of the ceremony, you come with the offerings and food. In some cases, an illness might take more than one night of ceremony, sometimes up to four nights. In that case, you must prepare offerings and food for each night of ceremony.

3. This red felt is a type of flag. It is called a *waluṫa*.

When the ceremony has been done, when things are better, you must put on a *wopila*, a thanksgiving ceremony. Again, you smudge and load your pipe and take it to the medicine man to tell him you want to put on a thanksgiving ceremony. Again, you prepare offerings and food, and the focus of the ceremony is on giving thanks for the help you have received. This is an important part of the entire process, and you must not forget to sponsor a ceremony to give thanks.

In preparation for any ceremony, you might also ask the medicine man who sings for him. If he gives you some names, it is helpful to contact those people and ask them to come. It's also good to show some kind of appreciation for the singers. These days singers are rarely gifted, and they provide the most important part of the ceremony.

Finally, after the each ceremony is done, we do what we call Wohoyake. This is the offering you give directly to the medicine man. Today it's mostly in the form of money, because that's how we live today. It can be some other gift as well, and sometimes people will give a blanket or a quilt, something like that, in addition to money. The amount you give is up to you, though the amount shows your appreciation. A real medicine man never gives you a figure or quotes a price for a ceremony; that's all up to you. If he's helped you, and you're truly thankful, you will give whatever you can. Wohoyake is always up to the individual, and there is no set amount. Sometimes people don't have anything. They have to struggle to get enough for the offerings and food, but the medicine man helps them anyway. If you can afford it, however, you compensate them accordingly. They really appreciate it.

Grandmother earth • Uŋčí Maȟa

The Nations of the Living Beings of the Earth • Wamakaśkaŋ Oyaŧe

Black Hills • He Saṗa

My relatives • Mitákuye

Prairie Dog nation • Pispiza Oyaṫe

Deer nation • Tahca Oyaṫe

Teacher • Waunste wicakiya

Moon • Haŋhepi wi.
*Wi* is a description of the sun or moon;
*haŋhepi wi* means "nighttime *wi*"
or "moon." *Aŋp̄eťu wi* means
"daytime *wi*" or "sun."

Horse nation • Śuŋḳa Waḳaŋ Oyaťe

My relatives • Miṫak̇uyeṗi

Sage • Ṗeji Hoṫa

Buffalo nation • Pte Oyate

Buffalo bull • Tataŋka.
Tataŋka is a description of the bull
buffalo. There are a few possible
derivations—it could mean "big
body"; also, ta could be short for tahca,
or "big deer." Taŋka means "big."

Grey buffalo horn • Pȟe Saŋ He

Horse nation • Śuŋka Waḱaŋ Oyaฺte

Relatives • Wotakuye
Eagle Nest • Wanbli Wahohฺpi

Black Hills • He Saṗa

Badlands • Makosica.
*Makosica* means "land
that is not good for living
or surviving."

Our relatives on earth and in the universe • Mit̄akuye Oyas'iŋ

Thunder nation • Wakiyan Oyat̄e

Deer nation • Tahca Oyaṫe

Toward where the sun
goes down • Wiohpeya Takiya

Horse nation • Śuŋ́ka
Wakaŋ Oya̅te

Coyote nation •
Śuŋgmani̅tu Oya̅te

Rainbow • Wigmuka

("Traps the sun")

# GLOSSARY

*Note: Some of these words or phrases will create an image or an action.*

Aḵanṯu Śni: *Aḵanṯu* means "visible" or "on top." *śni* means "not." Refers to the ones that are not visible. A term for spirits.

Aŋṗeṯu: Daytime or any day.

Aŋṗeṯu wi: Description of the sun; the shortened form is *aŋṗe wi*.

Aṯe: Father.

BIA: Bureau of Indian Affairs.

Ċaŋċeġa: A drum. Literally means "a wooden bucket." Before the familiar drum design came, the drum was a rawhide stretched out on sticks over a pit. Heated stones would be placed in the pit to tighten the hide. They used long chokecherry sticks instead of the drumsticks of today. They said the sound wasn't like the drums now but sounded really good.

Ċaŋḣṗaŋ Pizi: The color green. It is the color of the greenish sap from a tree. (Also *zito*: *zi*, "yellow," and *to*, "blue," so green.) On Rosebud, green is the color generally associated with the earth.

Ċaŋli: The generic term for tobacco. Tobacco is often mixed half and half with the dried light inner bark of the red willow, which is called Ċaŋ Śaśa.

Ċaŋli Waṗaḣṯa: These are tobacco ties. One-inch or so squares of cotton cloth usually in the colors of the six directions with a pinch of tobacco tied up in each cloth. The ties are made on a continuous string. Different spirits will ask for different numbers or colors: a spirit might ask for six green and six blue ties, so you would make them that way on one string.

Whatever the spirit (or the medicine man for the spirit) requests is what you make on a single string. They are made as offerings to the spirits, and each spirit has a different set of tobacco ties that is requested.

Ċaŋnup̄a: Description of any pipe.

Ċiŋkśi: Son.

Ċuŋkśi: Daughter.

Haŋbleċeya: Originally, this was *woihaŋble oweċeyap̄i,* "crying for a dream." Today it is shortened to *haŋbleċeya,* "vision quest."

Ḣaŋte: Cedar, or cedar tree.

Heyoḳa Woze: Contrary doing a kettle dance. A ceremony done by Heyoḳa.

Huŋḳap̄i: Ceremony done to renew a relationship. Can be between two parties or two people to renew relationship and harmony. Since reservation times, the people have used this ceremony for naming and making relations.

Ḣuŋwiŋ: Something that is spoiled and smells bad.

Ikċe Wiċaśa: Common man, ordinary man.

Ikṫomi: The generic term for all spiders, it is also the term for the trickster. There are many stories concerning the tricks Ikṫomi pulls on living beings, including humans. These stories are often funny and also teach us that we all have this spirit in us. We all have a tendency to be shrewd and manipulate others. Ikṫomi stories are often wild and exaggerated, and some concern pretty harmful behavior, how he tricks people into really bad situations. If we're not careful, however, we can do the same thing, so we tell these stories to caution against that.

Ina: Mother.

Inip̄i: They are bringing in new life, physically and spiritually. *I* refers to the energy or resource, *ni* means "to be alive," and *p̄i* is the plural form.

Iŋyaŋ: Creator and/or stone. Iŋyaŋ created by using his blood for each creation until creation was completed. Iŋyaŋ got dry and brittle and scattered all over the world. The stone is a remnant of Iŋyaŋ.

Iśnati: Living alone. Coming-of-age practice for young women. This is a ceremony done for the first few months after a young girl experiences her first monthly period.

Iṫoḳaġa ṫakiya: South. *Iṫe* is "face," and *oḳaġa* is "the place where they make the face," so "toward where they make the face," "toward where we face." Southern tribes use a mask for ceremonies, so it means "toward the place where they make these faces" (this definition is still under discussion but for now is current). White (*sḳa*) is the color generally associated with this direction on Rosebud.

Iyesḳa: Interpreter or translator. Contemporary term to describe the role of a medicine man.

Lila: Really, or very.

Lowaŋpi: They are singing. Code-talking description of a healing ceremony conducted by a medicine man during the time from 1880 to 1978 when all of our spiritual ceremonies were outlawed by the US Congress.

Maka: Earth, or dirt.

Maka Sitomniyaŋ: All around the earth. *Maka* is "earth." *Sitomniyaŋ* refers to "all around the earth, all over the earth." In prayer people sometimes use this term in praying for all creation on earth.

Maka Takiya: Toward the earth. Green (*zito*, or *caŋhpaŋ pizi*) is the color generally associated with this direction on Rosebud.

Mitakuye Oyas'iŋ: All my relatives. *Mitakuye* means "my relatives." *Oyas'iŋ* means "all."

Olowaŋ: A song.

Opaǵi: A pipe that is loaded with tobacco and ready to be offered or smoked.

Otiwota: Birthplace.

Owaŋka: Designated place for different activities, ceremonies; sun dance grounds, pow wow grounds. (Our term *hocoka* means the center. It is the same thing.)

Peji Hota: Sage. *Peji* is "grass," and *hota* is "gray," so "gray grass." A description of the sage we burn to repel the negative. It helps to clarify the mind when we burn and smell it. The smoke purifies the space and clears the area of any negative energy.

Pte hiŋcala caŋnupa: Buffalo calf pipe. *Pte* is "buffalo," *hiŋcala* is "calf," and *caŋnupa* is "pipe."

Ša: The color red, or adornment. *Luta* is another word for red. On Rosebud, red is the color generally associated with the North.

Sapa: The color black. On Rosebud, black is the color generally associated with the West.

Siŋte Gleška: Spotted Tail, Sicaŋġu leader who lived from 1823 to 1881. Siŋte Gleška University in Mission, South Dakota, is named after this important Sicaŋġu leader.

Siŋte Sapela: The black-tailed deer. *Siŋte* is "tail," and *sapa* is "black." *La* is an expression of endearment. Some of these deer have black on the tips of their tails and look like they have a mask. They have the power to communicate with humans. These are the *siŋte sapela*.

Šiyo taŋka: An eagle-bone whistle, or a flute. In the dictionary the definition of *siyo taŋka* is "big pheasant." *Šiyo* is "pheasant," and *taŋka* is "big." It could also refer to a goose, which makes a sound similar to a flute.

Ska: The color white. On Rosebud, white is the color generally associated with the South.

Šuŋgmanitu: A wolf or coyote. *Šuŋg*, or *šuŋka*, is "dog." *Manitu* is "where there are no human inhabitants." The literal meaning is "the dog that lives in the place where there are no inhabitants, or in the wilderness" (this is an English description, however, as there is no concept of wilderness in Lakota culture).

Šuŋka: A dog. Any kind of dog.

Šuŋka Wakaŋ: A horse. *Šuŋka* is "dog," and *wakaŋ* makes it a dog that has the powers of *wakaŋ*. It is a doglike figure that is *wakaŋ*. They say that a scout returned to camp long ago and said he'd seen a dog that was *wakaŋ*. People went to see it, and it was a horse. We still use that description for a horse.

Šuŋka Wičaša: Monkey. It describes a doglike figure that behaves like a human.

Takiya: Toward.

Tataŋka: A bull buffalo, or a big deer.

Tate: Originally, this was the part of creation that was the breath for life on earth. Today the wind is described as *tate*.

Tatuye Topa: The four directions of the wind. This term is used often because you make your appeal known to all the relatives in the four directions of the wind.

Tawačiŋ Waŋjila S'e: Be as of one mind. In a ceremony, after everyone expresses their need or appreciation, the medicine man will use this term to tell participants to put their minds together and think as one.

Tiošpaye: A small group that lives together. *Ti* is "to live someplace," and *ošpaye* is "a small group from the main group."

Tiwahe gle: Tiwahe gle is like an established home, where a family lives.

To: The color blue. On Rosebud, blue is the color generally associated with the direction above us, the sky.

Tuŋkaŋ: Sometimes the stones are called *tuŋkaŋ*. It means "from the beginning of time to now."

Tuŋkašila: *Tuŋ* is "birth," *kaŋ* is "old age," *ši* is "a relative," and *la* is an expression of endearment. A term of respect addressing any creation, physically or spiritually, that is very special. It says you represent the beginning of time to today, and you are dear to me. A term of respect for relatives: when the spirit of the eagle comes into a ceremony, it would be addressed as Tuŋkašila. Also, it could be an elder man of wisdom. This word is used to refer to a male figure, physical or spiritual.

Uŋči: A grandmother. They are the keepers of our traditions and history.

Uŋmašike: I have a particular need, and I know what this need is. The church translated this as 'I'm pitiful'. This is important to note, because today many of our people believe that they are essentially pitiful. We went back to the original meaning because the church translation so negatively affected how our people think about themselves.

Uŋšimala: Help me with a specific need. Saying I have a specific need, and I need help with that. *Uŋšimalayo* is the masculine ending if a man is asking for help. *Uŋšimalaye* is the feminine ending. They are both from the root word *uŋšimala*.

Waċaŋġa: Sweetgrass. A grass that grows in marshy areas and has a fragrant, sweet odor. Used in our ceremonies as an incense.

Waċaŋtognake: Generosity. *Ċaŋte* means "heart." *Ognake* means "you put something into your heart." This is the Lakota description of the English word *generosity*.

Waċekiye: To embrace or welcome a relative.

Wagluhtatapi: A ceremony to feed the spirits of the deceased. You feed them, and they help you in return. In the beginning Lakota people were instructed to do this ceremony. After they received the pipe, we decided to keep this ceremony along with the pipe. That is why we do both today.

Wagmuha: A gourd. The gourd or rattle used in ceremonies. *Wagmu* is "a melon," and *ha* is "the skin of a melon."

Wakaŋ: *Kaŋ* is "life or energy." Energy that can give life or take life. Energy that can be used for creation or destruction. Good and evil are within this energy and both are equally powerful. *Wa* is any creation that has *kaŋ*.

Wakaŋ Taŋka: When missionaries described God, that he created everything, that he created good and evil, they said he must be *wakaŋ*. They said his powers were big (*Taŋka*), so as a result *wakaŋ taŋka* usually refers to the Christian God. In Lakota thought, however, when you put all creation on the earth and in the universe together and include yourself, then that is Wakaŋ Taŋka.

Wakaŋyeja: An infant born with everything that is *wakaŋ*. Every newborn is *wakaŋ*. There is a need for care, as the new mind is fresh and soft and can be easily molded in any direction. The first five years are very important, and a child will spend the first five years of life with its mother and grandmother to learn an understanding of human emotions. A child is never weaned; it might nurse up to age four or five and will wean itself. If a boy grows up under that system, he will never abuse women. He will always have respect for them.

Wakiċuŋza: It is like taking an oath of office, making a vow or promise, a commitment. A sun dancer who pledges to dance is *wakiċuŋza*.

Waluṫa: A quarter-yard piece of red felt with a bundle of tobacco tied into one corner. Similar to *wouŋye* and made as an offering to the spirits.

Wamakaṡkaŋ: The living beings of the earth. All of creation on earth.

Wanaġi: *Naġi* is "a spirit." *Wa* refers to the spirit, to one of the creations that has that *naġi*. When a human dies, the spirit that leaves the body is a *wanaġi*. Any being that dies has a spirit that lives on, and *wa* refers to us, humans, as one who has that type of spirit. In English the word is *ghost*; in Lakota it refers to a being that has a spirit that lives on after death.

Waŋbli Gleṡka: The spotted eagle. *Waŋbli* is "eagle." *Gleṡka* is "spotted."

Waŋkaṫakiya: Above. Toward the sky, the stars, moon, sun, and so on. In the direction of the powers of the universe. Blue (*to*) is the color generally associated with this direction on Rosebud.

Waziya taḵiya: North. Where the *waziya*, the power of the North, resides. *Waziya* is considered life-giving or life-threatening power. They say that cleansing energy comes from the North. When Christmas was introduced to us, we were told that Santa Claus lived at the North Pole, so we called him Waziya. Red (*ṡa*) is the color generally associated with this direction on Rosebud.

Wiċaṡa ċehṗi: Man's flesh. *Wiċaṡa* is "man," and *ċehṗi* is "flesh."

Wiċoh'an: Traditions, rituals.

Wiċozani: Wealth. Based on physical and mental health, in balance with life and happy. Nothing to do with material wealth.

Wigmuka: Rainbow. Literally, this word means "traps the sun."

Wiohiyaŋṗa ṫakiya: East. Toward the light (*ohiyaŋṗa*) of the sun (*wi*). Toward where the sun rises. Yellow (*zi*) is the color generally associated with this direction on Rosebud.

Wiohṗeya ṫakiya: West. Toward where the sun goes down. Black (*saṗa*) is the color generally associated with this direction on Rosebud.

Wiwaŋg Waċiṗi: The sun dance. *Wi* is "the sun," *waŋg* is "to see" or "observing" (from the word *wayaŋg*), and *waċiṗi* is "they are dancing."

Wohoyake: The offering of compensation given to a medicine man. Whatever is given, the value demonstrates how much the ceremony is appreciated. It's a way of saying thank you. A medicine man will accept gifts but will never charge for a ceremony; it's up to the one being helped to determine the compensation. In a ceremony, offerings are made to the spirits, and in addition, compensation is given to the medicine man. Long ago a man would give his best horse in return for a healing ceremony, a gift as valuable as a pickup truck today. This is a concept that is much misunderstood today. People criticize medicine men for accepting money, for instance, but think nothing of paying a surgeon whatever is asked for an operation. Among Lakota today, I think it's due to the dependence that was created through western education and religion; our reservation systems are all designed to foster this dependence. We're conditioned to expect welfare, something for nothing. A true medicine man will not charge for his ceremonies, but he should be compensated appropriately.

Woksaṗe: Wisdom. Wisdom is knowledge and experience combined.

Wolakoṫa: Peace. Harmony with all creation.

Wo'ohiṫika: Bravery or courage. We say the most courageous act is to make a decision and then take responsibility for it. It is also used in reference to warriors or warfare, but the most important aspect of *wo'ohiṫika* is having the courage to make a decision.

Wo'oṗe: Natural laws that come along with any ceremony (or a gift from the spirits giving these laws). Traditionally, these are natural rather than man-made laws. Today, however, it is sometimes used for laws and policies.

Wopila: She or he appreciates something. An expression of thankfulness.

Wouŋye: These are what we call flags. They are quarter-yard lengths of cotton cloth in the colors of the six directions, each about eight or nine inches wide. A bundle of tobacco (about the same amount that will fill one's *caŋnuṗa*) is tied into a corner of each cloth. These are used in our ceremonies as offerings to the spirits.

Wowaċiŋṫaŋka: Refers to having a strong mind. The virtue of fortitude. Endurance. Patience.

Wowaḣwala: Peace, serenity, calmness.

Yuwiṗi: They are wrapping something up. A ceremony, usually by invitation only, where the medicine man is wrapped up in a quilt, and the spirits will untie him. In this ceremony (and all our ceremonies), the intent is to focus on the need in the ceremony, not on one's personal needs.

Zi: The color yellow. On Rosebud, yellow is the color generally associated with the East.

Zuya: *Zu* is "the journey," or "the mission." This could be war, a journey of exploration, discovery, or some other mission. *Ya* means that you are on that mission, or that he or she is going on that particular journey.

# SUGGESTED READING/LISTENING LIST

John Around Him and Albert White Hat Sr., *Lakota Ceremonial Songs* (booklet and CD)

Dee Brown, *Bury My Heart at Wounded Knee*

Ella Cara Deloria, *Waterlily*

Vine Deloria Jr., *Custer Died for Your Sins*; *C. G. Jung and the Sioux Traditions: Dreams, Visions, Nature, and the Primitive* (edited by Philip J. Deloria and Jerome S. Bernstein); pretty much anything else by Vine Deloria Jr.

Joseph Eagle Elk and Gerald Mohatt, *The Price of a Gift: A Lakota Healer's Story*

Ronald Goodman, *Lakota Star Knowledge: Studies in Lakota Stellar Theology*

John G. Neihardt, *When the Tree Flowered: The Story of Eagle Voice, a Sioux Indian*

Mari Sandoz, *Cheyenne Autumn*

Luther Standing Bear, *Land of the Spotted Eagle* (this book is very detailed about child rearing and early-childhood development in our culture)

R. D. Theisz, *Sharing the Gift of Lakota Song* (book and CD)

James R. Walker, any unedited works you can find

Albert White Hat Sr., *Reading and Writing the Lakota Language*

Dan Wildcat, *Red Alert! Saving the Planet with Indigenous Knowledge*

Charles F. Wilkinson, *Messages from Frank's Landing: A Story of Salmon, Treaties, and the Indian Way*; *The People Are Dancing Again: The History of the Siletz Tribe of Western Oregon*

Severt Young Bear, *Standing in the Light: A Lakota Way of Seeing*

# INDEX